Derek Lambert, author of many international best-sellers, including, *Angels in the Snow*, *For Infamous Conduct*, *The Yermokov Transfer*, *Touch the Lion's Paw* (soon to be made into an exciting motion picture starring Burt Reynolds), *The Great Land* and *The Saint Peter's Plot*, lives with his wife and son in Ireland.

Derek Lambert

Don't Quote Me . . . But

Futura Publications Limited

A Futura Book

First published in Great Britain by
Arlington Books (Publishers) Ltd in 1979

First Futura Publications edition 1980

Copyright © Derek Lambert 1979

ISBN 0 7088 1710 6
Printed in Great Britain by
Hazell Watson & Viney Ltd
Aylesbury, Bucks

Futura Publications Limited
110 Warner Road
Camberwell, London SE5

*For Larry and Jean Goddard,
and, of course, the girls — Anne, Jayne and Sally*

FOREWORD

A journalist's working day is almost always illuminated by shafts of humour. This book is an attempt to extract and crystallise the humour from the experience of one cub reporter. Contrary to public opinion, in my experience reporters are as deeply concerned with ethics, accuracy and balanced assessment as they are with exclusives, exposures and sensations. These considerations are outside the scope of this book, which was written with but one humble and optimistic aspiration: to amuse.

I

The headmaster stared at me in disbelief and said: "I'm sorry, but I don't think I quite understand the question."

Panic! It was my first interview, my first day in journalism, the launching pad of a career in which I already envisaged an endless series of world scoops — and I had encountered a pillar of erudition who didn't understand basic English.

I cleared my throat and repeated the question scrawled on the pad balanced on my knee. "Do you consider, Sir, that a diet of fish enhances the capabilities of the brain?"

The disbelief expanded on his ascetic features. My lips began to tremble, a manifestation of nerves that, for several years, was to blunt the cutting edge of my interviews.

Pencil poised, I waited to record his reply in shorthand. I had so far mastered about a dozen shorthand outlines and wrote faster in longhand; but that wasn't the point.

"Mmmmm," he said.

A tic developed in my right eye.

At last he spoke. "Would you care for a cup of tea?" This was said as though tea was a recognised sedative for amiable lunatics who reached his inner sanctums.

I thanked him, reflecting that it had never been like this with Hollywood reporters — Humphrey Bogart, James Cagney and all the rest — who, with hats tilted at rakish angles and cigarettes stuck in the corners of their mouths, struck fear into the hearts of mobsters and crooked cops and, after phoning the city desk, met gorgeous girls in dark bars.

I didn't have a hat, my city desk was a trestle table in the attic of the *Dartmouth* (Devon) *Chronicle* offices and my gorgeous girl had recently expressed scorn for anyone earning a pittance of thirty shillings a week. But I did possess half a Woodbine in the pocket of my raincoat. With considerable panache I lit it and coughed violently in the headmaster's face.

The tea arrived. We drank from delicate china cups adorned with roses and stared at each other. "Mmmmm," he said, "the relationship between intelligence and, ah, piscivorous habits." He cracked his knuckles still hoping, perhaps, that he had misheard the question.

He hadn't. Apparently the schoolchildren of Brixham had fared better in examinations than Dartmouth children and, because Brixham is a fishing port, it had occurred to my editor that the answer must lie in the fish.

"Get the story, laddie," he had grunted from his seat at the trestle table. He was an elderly, rotund, monosyllabic, acerbic Scot; but he was ex-Fleet Street and therefore a god.

The schoolmaster who taught in Brixham said between sips of tea: "I suppose it's possible."

There was a long silence while I recorded this tentative confirmation of my editor's theory. Pretty decent of him really because he could have elaborated at horrendous length while I puzzled over the shorthand outline for *possible*.

Now the follow-up question which I had been dreading because there was no telling what his first answer would be.

"Why?" I asked.

His wife came into the study with a plate of digestive biscuits. "Help yourself," he said.

The headmaster and I listened to my stomach whining with gratitude.

"Why?" he repeated my question.

"Yes, Sir, why?"

"Well," he said, "I'm not a medical man."

"I fully understand that." The biscuit was making my mouth dry. "But we have established that there is a relationship . . . "

"Have we?" he asked in surprise.

"I thought — "

"I only said it's possible."

"Ah."

I could see the headline: SCHOOLMASTER HINTS ON POSSIBLE LINK BETWEEN FISH AND BRAINS.

Perhaps the *Daily Express* or *Mirror* or *Mail* or *News Chronicle* would be interested.

"It would seem," I ventured, "that your pupils have done rather better in their exams than the Dartmouth children."

"Perhaps they're more intelligent," he said. He raised a hand to stop me. "Because of fish? Well, of course, the theory's not new . . . "

Instant deflation. A sensation to which I would become accustomed as an exclusive story was deposited on a carpet only to be pulled from beneath my feet by the discovery that it was old, that it contained an irreparable flaw in logic, that it was a pack of ingenious lies.

But he was a kind man, this chalky-fingered headmaster, and I'm sure that he produced generations of men and women well adjusted to such cruel blows of fate. He pointed out that, although the theory wasn't new, it hadn't received all that much publicity; and then asked in his kindly way how long I had been in journalism.

Well, not all that long . . . About an hour and a half to be precise. I told him that this was my first assignment.

"Then we must see what we can do," he said, consulting an

13

encyclopaedia. "And it wouldn't be the first time that an old story has been resurrected, now would it?" He found what he was looking for and began to read aloud, but neither my shorthand nor my longhand could cope with the dietary properties of fish and after a while he handed me the volume.

When I had finished making notes he asked if I thought I had got a story. Well, if a story was a list of chemicals and their properties, and an indefinite confirmation that fish *might* have something to do with Brixham brains, yes, I had a story. But not one to send James Cagney dashing to the phone.

He said: "Well look at it this way. You have two indisputable facts: the inhabitants of Brixham do eat a lot of fish and their children have done better in their examination results than the children of Dartmouth. Added to this you have some data on the mineral properties of fish. Now let us say that some of those minerals are contained in the nerve tonics that are available at any chemists then surely, at the very least, you have a thesis . . . "

I thanked him. I stood up. I had a story. I wanted to get to a typewriter. Hold the front page.

He saw me to the door and I heard the crack of his knuckles as I walked down the garden path. I wished that I had been taught by him instead of some of the sadistic pedants employed at my public school.

I hurried back towards the offices of the *Dartmouth Chronicle* which lay in the centre of the little town, beside the boat float, a hundred yards from the River Dart and the premises of W.H. Smith, where the papers containing my scoop would soon be on sale hot from the press (if it hadn't broken down again).

The headmaster's house lay high on the hills that cradle the town. On the flanks of the hills, terraces of houses and wandering alleys led like stepping-stones to the shops, pubs and ships. It was only February but the day was warm and fresh with a

14

breeze coming in from the sea. There were violets and snow-drops in the gardens, brass and copper winked brightly from behind bay windows; below me coins of sunlight floated lazily in the mouth of the Dart. The day smelled of childhood and, at the same time, excitingly of the future.

I reached the offices in the hold of an old building which was one of a row of buildings with shops and cafes beneath them, all "steeped in history," as I was frequently to describe the antiquities of South Devon.

An alley led under the building to the printing works where the old flat-bed was, under protest, thumping out posters advertising a gymkhana. I climbed the wooden stairs, knots polished brightly by the shoes of my predecessors, to the attic where at the city desk the editor sat chewing meditatively; he was always chewing although I never discovered what it was he chewed.

He grunted at me as I sat at my desk — the only desk — and slid a sheet of paper into the elderly Underwood. I stared at the sheet of paper, I consulted my notes. Gibberish. Symptoms of panic began to assemble.

Was my career to be stifled at birth? Another link in a natural progression which began with an undistinguished scholastic record, followed by ten months in a bank where I lost fifty pounds worth of travellers cheques and broke the lift, and two inglorious years in the medical service of the RAF.

I tested the typewriter. *Now is the time for all good men to come to the aid of the party*. The spacing was faulty so that wide open spaces appeared in the middle of some words whereas other letters were squeezed together like lovers.

I picked out the letters with two fingers, carefully and as slow as charity. Behind me I could hear the cud-like chewing of the editor who was writing an editorial.

In Brixham, I wrote, *the education authorities have been astonished*

15

by the excellence of the examination results in the town's schools.

Behind me the chewing grew louder. I glanced round and saw Sellar-Hay standing behind me peering over my shoulder, blue eyes as bright as diamonds in his plump Scots face.

He nodded wisely. Then pulled the sheet of paper from the typewriter and tore it in half.

He said: "Ne'er begin a story wi' a place or a time or quotes. Didna they teach you that in your correspondence course?"

I shook my head.

"Aye, well they wouldna I suppose," consigning any form of class-room training to the spike. There was only one road to success, the long hard road of experience, the road he had taken. "Och, laddie, you've got to have impact in that first paragraph, in the first word if ye can. Times, dates, places . . . they slow it up."

His advice, most of it good, some of it bad, has stayed with me just as first impressions are printed on a baby's brain. If I read a news story that begins *At 4.25 on Thursday afternoon* I believe, perhaps unfairly, that the author is an amateur.

He taught me many things did that arrogant old man, feared by his staff and the citizens of Dartmouth as a feudal landlord is feared by his serfs. He crammed into me a lifetime of cynical experience which had culminated before he headed for the West Country as a sub-editor on the *Daily Mail*. Mind you, he had his stylistic quirks: you could not have a *disaster* unless more than twenty were dead, you were not permitted *dramatic developments* — "If the facts are dramatic enough let the bluidy things speak for themselves" — and for some unfathomable reason you could not record that a meeting was *poorly attended* even if the audience consisted of two vagrants sheltering from the rain.

I rolled a second sheet of paper into the Underwood and stared at it hopelessly. My brain had seized up; perhaps I hadn't been eating enough fish.

A growl from behind me. "Wha's the point of the story, mon?"

"The connection between brains and fish," I said.

"Aye. And wouldna most people like to be more brainy?"

"I suppose so."

"Well tell 'em so, d'ye ken?"

Dimly I kenned.

"The personal approach. Get yon reader involved."

I stared desperately around the attic with its piles of yellowing newspapers, guillotine for cutting paper, reference library consisting of an out of date *Pears Cyclopaedia* and half an *Oxford Dictionary of Current English*. Sunlight beckoned through a dusty skylight.

I pecked out a sentence. *If you want more brains eat more fish.*

He was behind me again. "Aye, no' bad. Now attribute it."

To whom, for God's sake? *This theory has been given substance by examination results in Brixham.*

He handed me a scrap of paper on which he had scrawled in barely legible writing: *If you want more brains eat more fish — this is the message from the schoolchildren of Brixham.*

"Now finish it," he commanded, returning to his chewing and a virulent attack on the town council for some item of expenditure, any form of spending bringing out the worst in him.

I finished the story and handed it to him. With the stub of a pencil he subbed it, performed savage surgery, cutting paragraphs, simplifying sentences, obliterating lengthy dissertations from the headmaster's encyclopaedia.

"I suppose it will have to make do," he finally remarked staring at the mutilated copy. "But tha' correspondence course o' yours — dinna they tell you aboot writin' a story so it can be cut anywhere on the stone?"

17

I shook my head.

"Aye, well they wouldna I suppose."

We took the story down to the operator of the Linotype in a corner of the print shop. He was a sharp-faced, chain-smoking man who spent his working life converting words into slugs of gleaming hot metal. He was very fast, very competent, and showed signs of irritability only when visitors invaded his cocoon of cigarette smoke to ask if they could have their names set in type.

Half an hour later I had the wet proof of my first news story in my hand.

"Now proof-read it," commanded Sellar-Hay.

But my correspondence course hadn't said anything about proof-reading. Aye, well they wouldna I suppose. And what would the unions say if they heard that a journalist was encroaching into proof-readers' territory? But the unions seemed to wield little influence in this outpost of the fourth estate. Perhaps because Dartmouth was so inaccessible — they were talking about building a bridge over the Dart in those days and they are still talking.

He tossed me another proof he had already corrected and I set about indicating capital letters, fishing out misplaced slugs of type and correcting literals in my very own story. The classic literal that escaped a proof-reader's eye occurred, according to legend, in *The Times*. A reporter had described Queen Victoria passing over a certain London bridge. Unfortunately an "i" was substituted for the "a" in passing and, so the legend goes, all copies of the newspaper were recalled.

I handed the editor the corrected proof. He eyed it keenly. "Is that all, laddie?"

I said I thought it was, sensing that it wasn't.

"Read yon first paragraph again."

If you want more fish eat more brains . . .

I heard a noise like water passing through a rusty pipe. The editor was laughing.

II

A Devonian named Joe was largely responsible for ensuring that I got to work on time. He lived next door to my parents' home in a cul-de-sac of small houses high above the seaside resort of Paignton. He was a jovial, russet-faced man, passionately in love with his motor-cycle.

Most weekends he teased and fondled it, fed it with oil, and lay beside it dismantling its most intimate parts. And it was he who transported me every morning to Paignton, calling to me from the dawn-dark of his garden as I sat down to breakfast. Onto the pillion I would go, toast and marmalade in hand, unknotted tie blinding me as we tore down the hills past the waking houses towards the sea.

He deposited me outside the railway station where other workers were assembling with the sleepy cameraderie of early risers, coughing on the first cigarettes of the day while the man at the news kiosk cut the coarse string from the bundles of newspapers brought from London on the night train.

I imagined the scenes in Fleet Street as the deadline for these early editions approached. Men with green eye-shields, shirt-sleeves hoisted, frantically putting the paper together as the hands of the clock on the wall inched towards the witching hour. I smelled newsprint and printer's ink, and saliva flowed.

If I could afford it, if, that is, I hadn't been wildly extravagant with my thirty shilling salary, I bought a paper and read stories under great names — Sefton Delmer of the *Express,* Noel Barber of the *Mail,* Cassandra's column in the *Mirror.* Wars, murders, scandals ... One day, perhaps, the date-lines would be mine, but first I had to file an exclusive on the decline of lobster fishing in the village of Beesands.

Each morning I was joined on the platform by a middle-aged printer named Arthur, as dry-witted as he was thirsty.

The level-crossing gates opened, the train burrowed into the station, we climbed aboard and headed west. Past beaches where the ghosts of last summer's holidaymakers still lingered, past the waters of Torbay where small, mannered waves lapped the shore — or giant rollers savaged it — cross-country to the Dart where the track ran parallel with the river. On one side wooded slopes climbed to the sky, on the other yachts and skiffs and barges lay at rest in the mist while fish plopped and seagulls called to the dead.

The railhead was Kingswear, sister of Dartmouth, the family divided by the river. A cluster of fishermen's cottages and noble houses becalmed in the past — until the holiday-makers arrived, their cars queuing up the hill waiting for the ferry which crossed and recrossed the Dart as regularly as a pendulum.

Here we boarded the passenger ferry, a sturdy tug of a boat named the *Mew.* We gathered on the decks with the other regulars who had come west with us: a solicitor's clerk, a dissolute hotel porter said to have come from a titled family, the girl from the cake-shop, the librarian, workers from the Dartmouth shipyard, and a beautiful girl in a floppy hat with whom I was in love.

Ropes splashed, water churned, dead crabs and seaweed surfaced from green depths. To the right the battlements of Dartmouth Royal Naval College, ahead the bowl of Dartmouth, chimneys smoking, houses tossed on the hillsides where they had lodged, and to the left the open sea.

The year was 1949, I was twenty and this was my city, my metropolis, its stories waiting to be unearthed by a vigilant, incorruptible Pressman. Perhaps today an exposure of graft (Beesands' lobsters momentarily forgotten) that would shake the Establishment to its foundations.

Sellar-Hay was waiting in the attic, chewing. Forget Beesands, he said. He sent me instead to a funeral.

* * *

Funerals were unrewarding assignments

Only if the deceased (a banned word in the *Chronicle*) were a local dignitary could you hope to get the story across a couple of columns. And even then there were pitfalls as deep as graves.

The most hazardous of these was the list of mourners. People honouring the dear departed are very particular about the order in which their names are published. Promote an aunt from one family above an aunt on the bereaved's side and you're in trouble.

In the interests of accuracy I had to stand at the gate to the cemetery in the rain — it always rains at funerals — and thrust my notebook under faces bleak from their brush with death and demand names, making sure it was Smith and not Smythe, while the rest of the mourners shuffled dismally in the mud, awaiting their turn.

Often I had no idea that I would be dispatched to a funeral with the result that I arrived in my green herring-bone sports jacket patched with leather at the elbows and a red Paisley tie.

"I'm sorry, I didn't quite catch that," I would mutter, trying to hedge my insistence on accuracy with respect as rain-drops blurred my notes.

22

"Don't you know me, young man?"

"Sorry, ma'am, I'm afraid I don't."

"Hmpfff."

"I'm sorry but I'm a stranger round these parts."

"Hmpfffff." Why employ a foreigner?

Grudgingly they spelled out their names; but I wasn't finished with them yet. "Relationship?"

"Relationship?"

"To the deceased."

"Fourth cousin twice removed."

And can't wait for the will to be read, I thought, consigning her to the foot of the printed column.

The professionals knew better; they had visiting cards ready and, as they passed, they slipped them to me surreptitiously, like husbands over-tipping in the presence of stingy wives. These were the councillors, aldermen and businessmen who attended two or three funerals a year, taking them in their stride like Rotary Club lunches.

The sight of grief-stricken widows and widowers disturbed me. Love and security extracted from their lives as neatly and painfully as the pulling of a tooth, returning to cold beds and hollow futures. But I was not yet mature enough to put death in perspective; to understand that the living were merely waiting for the final reunion; so I adjourned to a riverside pub and drowned their sorrows in a half pint of shandy.

After taking their names at this, my first funeral, I returned to the office, wet trousers clinging to my legs, to sort out the pages of blurred nomenclature and sodden visiting cards.

A sheet of paper in the Underwood, Sellar-Hay looming behind. "Age," he grumbled. "How old was yon body? Always gi' ages, helps to identify . . . Yon body could be a babe in arms or centenarian. If ye ask a woman her age always make it your last question. If she won't tell ye add ten years on and she'll soon correct ye, d'yer ken?"

I kenned.

He read the second paragraph, then groaned as though stabbed from behind. "No, laddie," shaking his canny head. "Reverend, reverend?" as though repeating the name of a mortal enemy.

I stared at the paper. Well, yes, *reverend*. What in God's name had my correspondence course omitted to teach me about reverends?

"The reverend," he bellowed. "The, the, the. Always gi' them the article. Didna . . . ?"

"No," I said with dignity, "they didn't."

He retired to his trestle table shaking his head while I juggled with aunts and uncles and dear friends. How did you evaluate friendship in the hierarchy of mourners?

"And dinna forget the name of yon undertakers," Sellar-Hay muttered. "They advertise every week."

There was an alternative to all this agony, the printed form completed by the next-of-kin. This could be handed directly to the Linotype operator and we charged fourpence for every floral tribute. But these particular next-of-kin had spurned the printed form; perhaps they thought it was too clinical and perhaps they were right.

I tore out the sheet of paper and began again. *J.T. Mule.* Or was it *Male* or even *Mile?* I settled for *Mole.* A comforting little name from the pages of *The Wind in the Willows.*

I typed away with abandon. Settled back and read what I had written. I managed to tear it up just before Sellar-Hay attacked again from the rear.

He demanded to know why.

"It wasn't quite right," I said lamely because how could I tell him that, among the mourners, I had discovered the name of the deceased?

* * *

Gradually I began to feel the power of the Press. Local traders trying to insinuate free advertising in the guise of news — thwarted by the insertion of the item minus the name of the trader; convivial attempts over a pint of bitter to get a story killed — treated with arrogant disdain by me after I had drunk the bribe; requests at council meetings to the "gentlemen of the Press" to treat an item "with delicacy".

Gentlemen of the Press! Did anyone ever less resemble a gentleman? Sitting at the Press table, wild-haired, maniacally scribbling, six foot two inches tall wearing clothes tailored for a midget and sale-price shoes that looked like two small boats.

Sellar-Hay reported Dartmouth Council himself, writing shorthand at great speed on pads made from cut-offs from the guillotine. Members observed him warily — apprehensively when he suddenly drew two bold strokes beside an item in one of the committee minutes. The councillors were, perhaps, unlucky to have a Fleet Street vigilante thrust among them: Dartmouth was lucky.

He rarely made mistakes. But when he did he showed a marked aversion to apologising: if a retraction was unavoidable then it sometimes appeared disguised as another news story, or in the correspondence columns.

Some mistakes were such that an apology could only exacerbate the original mistake. Such as the occasion — not in my time — when the paper printed an account of the mayoral ball under the headline BIGGEST MAYORAL BALLS IN DARTMOUTH'S HISTORY.

A retraction might well have caused further offence. And in any case I'm sure that, as a result of the headline, many citizens viewed their civic leader with renewed respect.

While Sellar-Hay concentrated on Dartmouth Council, I

was dispatched to smaller and farther-flung councils armed with a handbook on local government, part of the correspondence course. From this I gathered that, whereas police and law courts had absolute privilege, i.e. you could report anything with impunity, council meetings had qualified privilege in which libel lurked shark-like beneath the verbiage. Nevertheless you couldn't miss a good story and when some farmer, crazed with cider, hurled abuse at the chairman because a scheduled sewer pipe would pass through his living room you had to be selective.

The parish council meetings were cosy affairs held in the village hall within a prayer's distance of the church and within ordering distance of the pub. Dogs barked outside, birds sang in the budding trees and there was always the possibility that in the middle of important business a wife would enter and announce: "Your supper's ready, George."

But, of course, these meetings were serious — the minutiae of democracy, their representatives attending rural district councils whose members attended county councils whose members travelled to London for full-blooded conferences.

And members treated them seriously, too, addressing each other as Mr. when, a few minutes later, they would be throwing darts together in the public bar of the Rose and Crown. School crossings, overhanging branches, drainage and sewage, floods and storm damage, repairs to the village constable's bicycle, a new bus shelter — this was the stuff of the evening in those antiseptic-smelling halls in the chiming villages of South Hams, as that part of Devon was known.

One particular council could always be relied upon to provide news. At Black Awton there was a nudist colony and there were constant complaints from both sides of the fence. Village worthies condemned the shameless display of naked flesh; the owners of the naked flesh complained about Peeping

Toms. Personally I couldn't understand it: the nudists enjoyed displaying their charms, the Peeping Toms enjoyed the display. Live and let live and surely the outraged worthies could look the other way. Nothing much was ever done about it and I suspected the answer lay in the gleam in the eyes of some of the more virile councillors.

Rural district councils were much more forbidding. And they provided me with a chance to meet reporters from daily and evening newspapers, representatives of the *Western Morning News* and *Torbay Herald Express* who actually *telephoned* their reports to copy-takers. (If the phone rang at the *Dartmouth Chronicle* it was answered by the elderly office manager who had an artificial leg; however, more often than not, by the time he reached the phone it had stopped ringing.)

These reporters made notes in beautifully lined notebooks while I scribbled furtively on a bunch of guillotined cut-offs stapled together. When the debate wasn't newsworthy they sat back and put down their pencils with quiet confidence while I relaxed beside them with spurious composure, mistakenly because the *Dartmouth Chronicle* needed all the news it could get — from applications to build allotment huts to repairs to public lavatories — and when we were short of copy I had to fill the blank spaces by writing letters for the correspondence column.

At Kingsbridge rural district council I was usually joined by Phil Ditton, of the *Western Morning News,* and a girl with magnificent breasts (fatal to my shorthand) from the Plymouth *Sunday Independent.* After the meetings we adjourned for a cup of tea to compare notes, a mortifying experience. When Phil Ditton, later of the *Daily Express,* and the girl from the *Independent* couldn't agree they consulted me. The three of us gazed blankly at my cut-offs, some bearing fragments of advertisements, covered with weird hieroglyphics and half-finished

27

words tapering off into straight lines.

When they were thus reduced to seeking the truth they usually decided to abandon the item altogether.

Humiliated, I returned to Paignton where once again my mother, a tireless tutor, guided me through Isaac Pitman's tortuous grammalogues.

Sometimes I attempted to take down the news from the radio. "This is the BBC Home Service" was converted into immaculate outlines. Thereafter the note-taking went into a sad decline with whole passages missed so that, when transcribed, it was not uncommon to discover the President of the United States presiding at the House of Commons.

*   *   *

Police courts provided the most formidable challenge to the raw cub reporter. But they were good for the ego — striding into court while friends and relatives of the villains noted your presence with respect, exchanging a few jocular words with the police sergeant; sitting at the Press table with theatrical aplomb; scanning the charge sheet; recording the names of prosecuting and defending solicitors; standing up prematurely to show your familiarity with court procedure as the magistrates filed in.

Then into the dock came the first of the villains. They were often a disappointment — a habitual drunkard fished out of the boat-float, a youth who had stolen a length of lead piping, a husband who had punched his wife in the eye because his dinner was cold. We were decidedly short on Crippens and Capones in the South Hams.

Sex cases livened things up a bit. The court was cleared of women who departed with marked reluctance. The Press could stay if they wished. We wished. Although we didn't have much to do except listen, because criminal sex was sparsely recorded in the newspapers in those days, and it was left to the imagination of the reader to identify the *certain offence* committed in the vicinity of the bandstand.

It was on occasions such as these that one became aware that magistrates were human.

I once covered a case when a garage owner was accused of selling pornographic films. He pleaded guilty and both prosecution and defence insisted that it wasn't necessary to see the movies.

The magistrates — a bank manager, a laundry proprietor and the owner of a gents' outfitters — nodded sagely. The chairman — the gents' outfitter, coffin-faced and funereally-garbed — said: "I think it would serve the interests of justice if we saw these films."

The prosecuting police inspector said firmly: "I don't think it's necessary, your worship."

The defending solicitor agreed. "I can't see that it would serve any useful purpose."

The chairman sought advice from the magistrate's clerk who vigorously shook his head; perhaps he had seen the films.

The chairman then consulted the bank manager and the laundryman. "We have decided," he announced after a few moments, "that in all fairness to the defendant we should see *all* the evidence."

The defendant, a wet-eyed, glossy-haired man of middle age shrugged.

The police inspector said: "But — "

But the chairman interrupted him: "We have decided."

And off they trooped to an ante-chamber to view the evidence. When they returned an hour later there was a new bounce to their steps and the bank manager was heard to murmur: "Quite disgusting," wiping his steamed-up spectacles.

The defendant was duly fined and the magistrates returned to their homes where, perhaps, astonished wives were invited to participate in activities the like of which they hadn't enjoyed since their honeymoons.

A fair and accurate report was the guideline at police courts. You had to give prosecution and defence an equal crack of the whip. And, unless you had an up-and-down guilty plea, this involved attributing facts so that it was not the *Chronicle* that asserted guilt.

Salvation lay in *alleged*. Everything was *alleged*. It was *alleged* by the prosecution . . . P.C. Smith *alleged* that the *alleged* offence occurred shortly after midnight — the hour when most alleged offences seem to occur. I used to scatter my copy with *allegeds* to the point where I was in danger of referring to the alleged magistrates.

Names, of course, were a perpetual source of harassment. If there were two F. Smiths in town it was disconcerting for the innocent F. Smith to read that he had been convicted of indecently exposing himself in the riverside gardens. It was useless to deny this to friends and neighbours. Outwardly they accepted the rebuttal but the expression on their faces said: "Always knew old Fred was a bit that way inclined." The only redress was a printed item in the paper. *Innocent F. Smith was not the F. Smith referred to etc.* But despite the correction the eyes of wary matrons strayed towards innocent F. Smith's fly-buttons as he walked his dog along the embankment.

The best precaution was to explicitly identify guilty F. Smith. Age, occupation and address with some additional identity tag such as *wearing a double-breasted Navy-blue suit and a maroon tie.* If innocent F. Smith chose to wear identical clothes then some power greater than the Press was exacting retribution.

My worst experience of mistaken identity occurred in a country police court where a thief had been caught stripping lead from the roof of the parish church. He had been spotted making his escape by the cleaning woman and had been picked up later by the police because he had a string of convictions as long as the list of Grand National runners.

The cleaning woman stood in the witness box, having declined the offer of a chair, arms akimbo, thin face alive with outrage.

The police inspector, resplendent in his best uniform, asked a routine question. "Can you identify the man you saw running away in court?"

"I can." She was adverse to elaborating.

"Ah. Can you point out that man to the magistrates?"

"I can."

"Then," said the inspector irritably, "Could you please do so."

"I could."

"Then please do so, madam."

She pointed unerringly at me.

The thief, fat and wheezing, the antithesis of anyone's idea of a cat burglar, grinned.

The spectators sat back for some fun. Next to the police, what better target for ridicule than the Press who set themselves up as arbiters of taste and justice?

The inspector was prevented by rules of judicial procedure from leading the witness. He could not say: "I'm afraid you are mistaken, madam." He could not say: "Is it the man in the dock?" The old harridan was his witness and he was stuck with her.

"Are you quite sure?"

"Quite sure."

"You couldn't be mistaken?"

She glared at him. "My eyes are as good as the day I was born. Better than yours I expect."

The chairman interposed. He was a humorous man, a great exponent of judicial ignorance, that laborious branch of comic inventiveness when a lawyer refers to, say, John Wayne and the judge says: "Who's he?"

This time the chairman contented himself with: "Please confine yourself, madam, to the question — this isn't an optician's."

Ingratiating solicitors sniggered.

The inspector said: "Cast your eyes once more around the court, madam. Now" — a sheen of sweat on his brow — "can you or can you not see the man you observed escaping from the church?"

She gave him a withering look. "I just told you, didn't I? That's him over there with the head of hair. I'd recognise him a mile off."

The inspector sighed. He was well-known for his courtroom style. A ruthless prosecutor, deadly in cross-examination, promotion but a few convictions away.

He appealed to the chairman. "I think that an adjournment might be in order."

The solicitor for the defence jumped to his feet. "With respect, I don't consider that to be in order at all." He was a young man with an unnaturally high-pitched voice. "With respect I am entitled to cross-examine this witness. It would appear to me that she has made a positive identification" — all eyes on me — "and merely because this doesn't assist the case for the prosecution it would be doing less than justice to my client if an adjournment were to be granted at this juncture."

The chairman said: "At this juncture, Mr. Brown? You make it sound like a railway station."

The inspector laughed heartily.

The solicitor said: "With respect, my client does not view his arraignment as in any way humorous."

A mistake. Always laugh at the ripostes of justices of the peace.

The chairman considered him for a moment, sunlight glinting on his pebble glasses. Then he said: "Mr Brown, an adjournment hardly precludes cross-examination."

Brown, promptly: "With respect, it interrupts it. It gives the witness time to consider her evidence."

The witness: "So I'm a liar, am I?"

Mr. Brown spread wide his hands.

The chairman's humour was deserting him. "Questions are the prerogative of the solicitors, madam."

"Is he entitled to call me a liar?"

"Be quiet, madam."

"I won't — "

"If you don't obey the ruling of this court I shall be forced to consign you to the cells for contempt."

The witness muttered something inaudible. The defendant stretched and yawned. The spectators moved restlessly. The magistrates conferred.

The chairman turned his attention to the Press table.

"Perhaps Mr . . . ?"

"Lambert," I said, hearing my voice as though it belonged to a stranger.

"Perhaps Mr. Lambert would be kind enough to stand up."

I stood up while my treacherous colleagues from other papers scribbled furiously. My cheeks were hot, my mouth trembled uncontrollably.

The chairman said to the witness: "Now, are you absolutely sure, madam, that this gentleman is the person you saw running away from the church?"

She stared at me and I stared back. "Well — "

"Is he or isn't he?"

"He's got the same hair but — "

33

"But what, madam?"

"He didn't seem as tall as that."

"Ah."

The defendant frowned, hand unwittingly straying to his own hair which was of the same unbridled calibre as mine.

The witness pounced. "That's him," pointing at the defendant as though he had been hiding. "I'd recognise him anywhere."

The chairman's good humour returned. "You may sit down, Mr. Lambert."

Unhappily for the defendant the prosecution's case did not depend solely on identification. He was sent for trial and got six months, accepting the sentence as stoically as he had accepted sentences in the past and would doubtless accept them in the future.

After the committal I returned home thoughtfully, wondering how many innocent citizens were languishing in gaol as the result of well-meaning but mistaken identity.

Next day I had a haircut.

III

Every Wednesday I was dispatched by double-decker bus on a news-gathering tour of the villages of South Hams. Hamlets pocketed among green hills, smelling verdantly of agriculture, cleansed by saline draughts from the sea. Stoke Fleming, Strete, Slapton, Torcross, Beesands . . .

"Gi' out there and get yon news, laddie," Sellar-Hay would intone and, after a two shilling lunch at a little cafe with red-chequered tablecloths down the road from the office, I boarded the bus beside the boat-float and took off with as much idea of collecting news as I had of navigating the *Queen Mary*.

Most books on how-to-become-a-journalist advocated chasing fire engines, ambulances and police cars. But I was handicapped by either being on top of a bus or on foot.

We had correspondents in some of the villages but their contributions were largely confined to church fetes and raffles in aid of causes of which they happened to be honorary secretary, and storm damage. Occasionally they struck gold with the rifling of an offertory box or the rescue by the fire brigade of a cat stuck up a tree. We paid them one penny a line for their contributions which perhaps explained why they didn't exactly scour the countryside for news.

So it was up to me.

"Always make for yon pub and post-mistress," Sellar-Hay

advised, hinting vaguely at unimaginable rustic decadence.

Which was all very well except that publicans didn't take kindly to inquisitive young men leaning on their bars without the price of a half pint in their pockets.

Sub-post-mistresses, however, were more fruitful, sitting behind their grilles issuing stamps and postal orders in shops that smelled of sherbert and tobacco where you could buy sepia postcards of local views, *John Bull*, *Everybody's* and *Lilliput*, bottles of lemonade and Tizer, aniseed balls and wafers of transparent toffee.

All things were known to these ladies and they could have blackmailed the whole village if they had been so inclined. But they weren't, so I had to make do with an all-night vigil over a cow in calf, vandalism in the telephone kiosk (always the work of visitors), a chimney fire or a holiday-maker stuck down a cliffside. From the publicans came the latest results in the dart league — and sometimes a free half of bitter.

Crime was in short supply, particularly in one village where the constable hadn't made an arrest for eighteen years.

He was a jovial man with cropped hair, vowels as round as apples, pink cheeks and a belly like a base drum. He was much liked and respected and ruled his tiny domain with the judgement of Solomon.

But in some bleak headquarters where the pageantry of life was studiously recorded in rulered ledgers they were gunning for him. It didn't matter a jot that the village was free of crime, surely the ultimate aim of law enforcement. All that mattered was the absence of arrests.

So a man from HQ arrived in the village and was closeted with the constable in his red-brick police house for two hours. When he departed the constable adjourned to the pub.

"Hallo, my old darling," he said to me. And to the landlord: "Pour the scribe a pint of his tipple."

By this time the constable had consumed several pints of scrumpy, the devil's brew of cider that sends the mildest of men barking into the night. The constable was in full lament.

"They be after me, scribe," he said. "They be out to get me. Seems we haven't enough villains in the village."

He pushed his empty tankard across the bar to the landlord who replenished it. No money exchanged hands, but the landlord had no worries about serving drinks after time.

"What are we'm going to do about it, my robin?" he asked me as I buried my head in a half pint of mild and bitter.

I thought about it. I was proud that he considered me as a confidant but I could think of nothing constructive to contribute.

The constable's usual method of dealing with anyone who disturbed the peace and quiet of the village was to bang their heads together or buffet them with his stomach. And such was his authority that a few growled words of warning were usually sufficient to curb any criminal aspirations.

He turned to the landlord, a thin man with grey hair pasted over his scalp. "What do you'm think, John?"

The landlord, envisaging police replacements and a tighter rein on drinking hours, shook his head gloomily and poured himself a large whisky. "Perhaps you could knock off a few grockels," he suggested. (To a Devonian a grockel is a holiday-maker.)

We ruminated on the suggestion.

"Ah, but it seems a mite unfair. Send 'em packing with a thick ear — has always been my method," and to me: "Know of any likely candidates, my old luv?"

Without asking, the landlord filled up my tankard. I wasn't used to drinking — how can you be on thirty shillings a week? — and my thinking was becoming wild; not only that but the last bus to Dartmouth was due.

The landlord said: "Might be unfair, but not if them were real villains who deserved it."

The constable considered this. "You'm got any real nasty bastards in Dartmouth, scribe?"

"A few," I said non-committally.

"Any that really deserve a spell inside?"

"I'll have a look around," I said.

The landlord regarded us shrewdly. "I'm going away for a week's holiday," he said.

We looked at him and he looked at us.

"The brewery's sending up a temporary to look after the place but the bugger won't be here at nights. The lock on the store's broken and I'm taking Jessie" — his Alsatian — "with me."

Outside I heard the bus moving off; somehow I had failed to hear it arrive. I chased it and managed to haul myself onto the running board.

Standing on the deck of the *Mew* that evening, and sitting in the train as it nosed its way through the dusk, I tried to think of someone in Dartmouth whom I would happily dispatch to prison. But anyone who deserved a stretch was already doing one.

I widened my scope around the shores of Torbay — Brixham, Paignton, Torquay, Teignmouth, Dawlish . . . Now here there were one or two roaming bands of witless young men who spent their leisure trampling on flowerbeds, sticking knives into motor-car tyres or breaking milk-bottles. Some of them also indulged in a little thieving.

I knew a couple of them vaguely, having interviewed them when they had been bound over at Brixham magistrates court for shop-lifting.

I met them one Saturday night in a sea-front pub at Paignton. Paignton was a gentle family place with a street of shops and ice-cream parlours, a pier, a population of seaside land-ladies and a beach where men in braces and handkerchiefs knotted on their heads sat in deckchairs as they had sat since their first holiday postcard was printed. It followed, therefore, that from time to time the sort of young man who liked to stamp on a child's sandcastle felt the need to liven the place up.

My two acquaintances were tanking up with beer prior to a livening-up session when I met them. I even bought them two halves reflecting that I would be able to make good the loss in the crime-free village hostelry.

I suppose I was aiding and abetting a crime but I casually let it be known that there was an Aladdin's cave of unguarded loot for the taking in the village. The weekend, I off-handedly implied, would be the best time to make a killing.

The following Saturday the constable took up his position in the darkened bar of the pub; from time to time his hand reached unerringly for his pint of scrumpy.

Shortly after midnight — what other time? — there were sounds of stealthy activity in the backyard.

Reluctantly the constable made his way into the yard and made his first two arrests in eighteen years. The two layabouts got short prison sentences and at HQ the constable's meagre score was duly chalked up.

The constable expressed his gratitude to me in the pub. But for a while he was a broken man; in his book a few sturdy butts with his belly, a couple of cuffs round the ear and a stiff lecture would have better served the course of justice than prison. Myself I doubted it: those two young miscreants had received their fair ration of kindness, and to them leniency was merely weakness.

Peace reigned in the village for another couple of years and no further arrests were necessary. The constable regained his confidence and exercised his benevolent authority until one day they once again consulted his record down at headquarters.

It really wasn't good enough, this total absence of criminal activity. It was unnatural. The constable was duly posted to an area with a high crime rate where even he could not avoid making the occasional arrest.

Shortly after his departure from the village there was an outbreak of robberies.

* * *

Gymkhanas, fetes and fruit, flower and vegetable shows in the villages helped fill many columns in the *Chronicle*.

I particularly enjoyed the horticultural shows. Wandering round the marquees, notebook in hand, grass churned into mint-sauce beneath my feet, inspecting the exhibits: long clean fingers of carrots and parsnips plucked from the red soil of Devon, nests of tomatoes and polished apples, bunches of dahlias with blooms as big as plates and chrysanthemums that smelled of autumn, home-baked cakes that slowly deflated, watched hopelessly by their owners.

There were dark deeds too, during and prior to the exhibitions. The colonel's marrow, for instance.

For as long as anyone could remember the colonel had always walked off with the first prize in the marrow section. It was really a non-event. Other gardeners watered and fertilised their marrows already accepting defeat because, whenever they peered over the colonel's hedge, their own gourds shrank to the dimensions of gherkins.

How did he do it? The colonel, a stiff-backed cantankerous old soldier with two ferocious Irish wolfhounds, was not popular and every year speculation was rife. Did he inject them with hormones? Did he possess some secret formula for

40

manure? Did he weave spells at the dead of night? It was even suggested that he blew them up with a bicycle pump.

Certainly the colonel wasn't telling. But every year, as summer spent itself towards autumn, a single green, glossy, white-ribbed marrow grew to gargantuan proportions amid yellow, cup-shaped blooms, and the colonel walked his growling dogs in the village with the hauteur of the victor towards those who would inevitably be vanquished.

Various methods of unearthing his secret were discussed. An all-night vigil was suggested but, with the approach of closing-time, enthusiasm waned. Attempts were also made to enrol the colonel's housekeeper as an informant, but she rejected all advances thereby ensuring scandalous rumours about her relationship with her employer.

And, like Topsy, the marrow grew and grew behind the privet hedge in the lovely old-fashioned garden stocked with hollyhocks, Sweet Williams and lavender in the shade of the colonel's ivy-coloured house built from bricks as mellow as Cheshire cheese.

I was present one evening in the public bar when the subject of the colonel's marrow once again surfaced.

"I be right fed up with that bugger," said Alf the carpenter, a chip-toothed little man who had once been a jockey.

Charlie the grocer, who was said to have been involved in the Invergordon naval mutiny, said: "I reckons we'm should blow the bluidy thing up."

The colonel had one supporter, a soft-haired bespectacled man named Albert who inscribed lettering on tombstones. "You'm all jealous," he observed, "just because he got a way with marrers."

This was received in silence until Alf, the ex-jockey who had a vicious streak in him, said: "It's your round, Albert, and I be partial to a little drop of whisky."

41

"There be something evil about that bugger's marrers," said Charlie who had given up the unequal battle and grew prize-winning ridge cucumbers on his allotment. "I mean them aren't natural."

"Like something out of science fiction," contributed the barman.

Albert polished his spectacles, ingrained with the dust from his gravestones. "Your trouble is you'm don't like competition. And you'm don't like foreigners winning neither." He had been born two villages down the road and hadn't yet been totally accepted. He bought a round of drinks as part of his campaign for acceptance.

"I reckon we should fix the bugger good and proper this year," said the ex-mutineer to whom the colonel represented commissioned authority.

But the council of war was cut short by the barman, who rang a bell with sadistic pleasure and called: "Time, gentlemen, please," and poured himself a glass of Guinness.

I stood up and made my way to the door to catch the last bus. As I left the ex-mutineer shouted after me: "And don't you'm go writing any of this or we'll have your guts for garters."

That night the wolfhounds were heard barking as though there were intruders. But the following morning the colonel was out walking the dogs in the sunshine and the marrow was still there like a cuckoo's egg amid the old English flowers.

The horticultural show took place on the Saturday. The judges patrolled the marquee while rain tapped on the canvas roof, stopping before each exhibit to make notes.

In the background exhibitors hovered anxiously. Not so the colonel: he sat comfortably on a shooting stick taking occasional sips from a silver hip-flask, confidence indelibly printed on his leathery features.

Now I suspect in retrospect that one of the judges had been

tipped off because it is not normal procedure to pick up an exhibit and examine it from underneath. However, with considerable effort, he did pick up the colonel's marrow.

And there, carved with beautiful precision, was a message suggesting what the colonel could do with his marrow — a physical possibility with a ridge cucumber, but certainly not with this monstrous vegetable.

The marrow was thereupon declared ineligible because it had been defaced.

The colonel immediately reported the defacement to the police and an inquiry was instigated. But village secrecy closed thickly around the affair, although much suspicion was directed against the former jockey and the ex-mutineer.

What struck me was the neatness of the lettering carved in the marrow's flesh — and the fact that thereafter Albert the stonemason was accepted by the villagers as one of their own.

IV

My only distraction from learning my trade was the girl on the ferry.

Beneath the floppy hat she had brown eyes and full lips and she laughed a lot, regrettably at the asides of a curly-haired young man with whom she worked at Dartmouth Pottery.

I was virtually penniless and she didn't look the sort of girl who would be satisfied with a tuppenny promenade along Torquay Pier; nor, I decided, would half a pint of scrumpy in the Hole-in-the-Wall be considered an adequate substitute for cocktails in the Imperial, the Grand or the Palace.

She disturbed my shorthand to the extent where I confused *love* with *loathe* (they are similar outlines), and made sausages of my fingers as they pounded the keys of the Underwood.

If I were a penniless artist it would be acceptable, such are the unfair advantages accorded to the arts; but a penniless reporter never. The reporter image is fine, but it has to be archetypal — I should have been standing on the deck of the *Mew,* hands deep in the pockets of a belted raincoat, coat-collar turned up, wise-cracking with some private eye; it was decidedly not archetypal to be standing there holding corned-beef sandwiches wrapped in grease-proof paper listening to a dirty joke recounted by my friend the printer.

Sometimes I was fickle enough to escape the companionship of the printer and stand at the rail of the ferry gazing out to sea, attempting to give the impression that, beneath the hack, there lurked the poet and praying that Sellar-Hay wouldn't think fit to put my by-line over the Brixham fish prices.

If I could possess some sort of title it might help. Admittedly I was chief reporter of the *Chronicle* but that is hardly impressive when you are also the only reporter. Author? Well, yes: I had recently written a one thousand word article on *How to Succeed in Journalism* for a magazine called *The Writer* for which they had paid me one pound; but I had blown that at the Spa Ballroom, Torquay, dancing with a girl who had leaped on the last bus to Babbacombe leaving me to walk home to Paignton.

All I could do was to look alternatively soulful and mysterious while the printer edged up and asked me if I'd heard the one about the girl in slacks and the Scotsman in a kilt.

At Dartmouth quayside every morning the girl tripped happily away in the direction of the pottery on the arm of the curly-haired potter while I made my way past the boat-float to meet Sellar-Hay.

But hope glimmered when Sellar-Hay decided to double the editorial strength under him. He appointed as junior reporter the sixteen-year-old son of a local fishmonger. His name was Terry Fleet and when I last heard of him he was an executive on Westward Television.

At that time he looked marginally less like Humphrey Bogart or James Cagney than I did. A likeable young man with brown hair and a cheerful face who, like myself, burned with determination to succeed. It is difficult to believe but I suppose he was paid less than me!

To Terry I imparted all my expertise: it didn't take long. But I was the old hand and suitably cynical with it, even though his shorthand was swifter than mine. He also had the advantage that he was local and a noted swimmer to boot, competing successfully in the boat float, a sort of miniature harbour where diving was restricted to high tide unless you wanted to bury yourself in mud.

After a while he was occasionally entrusted with the news-gathering run round the villages. Before he departed I took him aside for a cup of tea in the Bay Tree and told him: "Always make for the pub and the post-mistress."

But Terry's principal asset, as far as I was concerned, was that I now had staff under me. I was the chief reporter, albeit by a short head. Now was the time to make my play for the girl in the floppy hat and to hell with the curly-haired potter whose witticisms she seemed to find so inordinately funny.

I prepared the ground carefully. Twice I wrote features about the pottery. Sellar-Hay grumbled, suspecting I think that I was taking a back-hander from the owners of the pottery but, confronted by columns of open space, he printed them both.

I contrived to loiter near the bench where she was working, showing myself in the company of the managing director who engaged me in incomprehensible conversation about pottery. We acknowledged each other with polite smiles.

In the mornings I tried to get into the same train compartment as her. But this proved difficult because she lived at Torquay, the stop before Paignton. If she was at the front of the train I had to belt down the platform accompanied by the protesting printer; if we didn't make it we had to hurl ourselves into the nearest compartment as the train gathered speed. When we stationed ourselves at the far end of the platform her head would emerge from a window at the rear.

Nor was it much better when we managed to get into the same compartment where she would be esconced with the curly-haired potter who had already taken full advantage of the stretch between Torquay and Paignton to make her laugh uproariously.

"Good morning."

"Good morning." She smiled deliciously beneath the hat.

"Lovely day." With rain lashing against the windows.

"Mmmmm."

The potter murmured something in her ear and she giggled.

Time for the Chief Reporter of the *Chronicle* to strike. But first there was a diversion on the decks of the *Mew*.

The agonies of calf love were light years behind the printer and he treated my courtship with remorseless humour. This included making disparaging comments about the girl's hats. On one occasion he implied within earshot of the girl that I thought her hats were props from a pantomime. She stared at me with hurt brown eyes but, such is the conspiracy of bonhomie between men, I didn't contradict him; merely stood there with a fierce smile on my face, lips twitching as though they possessed a life of their own.

That morning in the police court not even a robbery at Dartmouth Castle could raise my spirits. And, when the motoring offences began, I took down the barest details. Motoring cases were the nadir of court reporting because it was difficult to impart zest into skid marks, road conditions and visibility. Their only interest was the vehement sincerity with which the protagonists gave totally conflicting accounts of an accident. There were, of course, exceptions to the rule such as the motorist who stole a car, bounced off seven parked cars, narrowly missed a policeman on a bicycle, climbed out reeking of alcohol and, when arrested, claimed that he was being victimised.

When I got back to the office there was a parcel awaiting me. Inside was a floppy hat smelling sweetly of her perfume accompanied by a note: *Hell* hat *no fury like a woman scorned.*

Was this the end of the beginning? Rapture and savage gloom alternated that afternoon. I smelled the perfumed hat and Sellar-Hay who had silently ascended the stairs said:

"What the hell d'yer think you're at, laddie?" looking at me as if I were a Sassenach pervert.

We had a messenger on the staff who also brewed tea as sweet as sugar-icing and next morning I dispatched him to the pottery with the hat wrapped in brown paper. Inside the hat was a note of apology signed *The Mad Hatter*.

That evening she was on the *Mew*. There was no potter in sight and the printer had repaired to the pub. The sky was dusk-mauve, the river was settling for the night beneath the silent woods.

There was nothing for it: I had to speak: we couldn't just stay there alone on the deck while I stood aloof like Napoleon on his way to St. Helena.

"Sorry about the hat," I said gruffly.

"That's all right. I knew it wasn't you anyway." She was wearing the perfumed hat, slightly crumpled from its journeying.

A pause. The bottomless treasure chest of the English language lay within my grasp.

"You're late tonight," I said after deep thought.

"I was finishing a design on a vase."

"Oh."

"And what were you doing? Following up a murder?"

She, too, was the victim of Hollywood as most young people were. I decided not to reveal that I had been reporting a rabbit show where I had been bitten by a vicious angora.

"This and that," I said.

We boarded the train at Kingswear and sat opposite each other.

She said: "What exactly is your position on the *Chronicle?*"

"I'm Number Two," I told her, refraining from explaining that, after me, there was Number Three and that was that.

"It must be terribly interesting."

"You see life," I said.

"I wish I had curly hair like yours," she said suddenly.

I pushed my fingers through my hair in which a pencil could lay hidden for weeks. "Yours suits you."

"Except when it's covered by a pantomime hat."

We both laughed. We relaxed, or at least I did because she already was. I should like to have ridden the train with her to Torquay but it was Thursday and I only had thruppence in my pocket which was hardly a passport to rapture.

"I wonder," I said carefully, "if you're doing anything tomorrow night." Friday was pay-day.

She thought about it, then said she wasn't.

"I thought perhaps we'd go to the theatre."

"That would be nice," she said.

Perhaps she imagined long-tailed jackets and gleaming shirt-fronts, ladies with marble busts fanning themselves beneath chandeliers, glasses of champagne in the interval.

But it wasn't quite like that. In return for publishing reviews of the shows at the Torquay Pavilion — reviews written by their own publicists — the *Chronicle* was allowed two free tickets a week. This week it was ballet, *Swan Lake*.

I met her outside the Pavilion, a regal old building from another age, green and white and domed and faintly oriental, with Torquay harbour behind it and gardens with a fountain and bandstand to one side.

She offered to pay for her ticket but, unfailingly gallant, I refused her offer because, after all, I hadn't paid for either of them.

But the trouble with the free tickets was that they were never the best in the house. We were placed directly behind a pillar. We saw the lead male dancer leap onto the stage from the wings and the ballerina enter gracefully from the opposite side and, by craning our necks, we saw them both exit; what happened in between was a mystery.

There were occasional thumps as the massive-thighed male dancer leaped about accompanied by bursts of applause from the audience; but we saw none of this, not even the swan dying. By the end of the first act we had finished the box of Cadbury's Milk Tray that I had bought after borrowing a pound from my father.

After the show we walked round the harbour for a drink at the Royal. And there was the curly-haired potter.

After one drink I suggested to the girl — her name was Maureen — that we adjourn to the Yacht and the curly-haired potter said: "Yes, what a good idea."

I thought it would be an even better idea if he bought a drink. Which he did because he was, after all, a likeable fellow; when he finally departed, leaving us together, I thought he was the salt of the earth.

When we left the Yacht it was raining. We walked round the harbour watching raindrops plucking at the water.

It must have been the two halves of bitter or the surfeit of Cadbury's Milk Tray or the intoxicating presence of the girl beside me but, as we approached the Strand, I was overcome by a bout of insanity: I hailed a taxi.

"Can you really afford it?" she asked.

Did Churchill smoke cigars! "Of course," opening the door for her.

In the taxi we held hands. Outside her home, with the rain falling gently upon us, we kissed. And then she was gone, but only for the night and before she went she told me what part of the train she would be in next morning.

I took the taxi round the corner where I dismissed it to save money. When I reached the sea-front the last bus to Paignton had departed.

I walked home. I ran, I leaped. It seemed that I was home in a couple of minutes, the taste of that first kiss in the rain still on my lips. And sometimes today it seems as if it's still there.

V

Editorial duties at the *Chronicle* were all-embracing. They included sticking wrappers round editions for postal delivery, sub-editing my own stories and taking down telephoned advertisements when the office manager had gone to lunch.

To me the most important advertisement was for the Maxime, the local cinema, because, as in the case of the Pavilion at Torquay, there were free seats to be had. The advertisements were accompanied by publicity hand-outs for each film detailing the brilliance of directing, acting and photography. If I had seen the movie I sometimes tempered the fulsome praise by inserting such scathing comments as: *A rather less-than-convincing performance was given by . . .* " But I never did a Kenneth Tynan or a Bernard Levin: I appreciated those free seats in the stalls.

But it wasn't the reviews that put paid to those pleasurable hours in the celluloid darkness: it was the advertisements. It was as if each of us who touched the ads — Sellar-Hay, Terry Fleet, the office manager and myself — was guided by some malevolent force. We were powerless to get them right.

On one occasion we got all the times wrong so that anyone wanting to confine themselves to the main feature had to sit through an interminable "B" picture, a cartoon, a travelogue, the March of Time, Movietone News and trailers for next week's programme.

Sometimes we got the actors in the wrong movies. Shirley

Temple starring in *Tarzan of the Apes* was my most memorable error. Sometimes we got the category wrong asserting that *Scarface* was a "U" movie fit for all the family.

All of this hurt Sellar-Hay where it hurt him most — in the pocket — because every publication day the cinema manager would telephone, patiently point out our mistakes and suggest that next week's advertisement should be inserted free.

Every week we perused the advertisement. Handed it to each other for second and third readings. But the printer's devil was abroad and the clangers appeared as regularly as the phases of the moon.

Eventually the patience of the cinema manager had to be exhausted ...

Advertising copy and publicity hand-outs always arrived well in advance. A double feature for the children — *Bambi* and *Snow White and the Seven Dwarfs* — was scheduled. I wrote heart-warming reviews, we checked and double-checked the advertisement. Into the paper went reviews and advertisement.

On Monday afternoon the children queued for the show while their parents retired gratefully for an afternoon of leisurely recreation.

But this mutual happiness was not to be realised. There was indeed a double-feature at the cinema — *Dracula* and *Son of Frankenstein*.

Next day the manager cancelled the advertisement — and my free seats in the stalls.

* * *

Another fringe journalistic activity was filling up the blank spaces with letters from readers.

Such malpractices were not uncommon in those days and I recall a six foot five inch reporter who wrote a weekly column about rugby and signed himself Oval Ball. Not only that but he played rugby himself and every other week Oval Ball would suggest that it was about time he was picked to play for the county. Eventually he was selected and made such a dismal showing that even Oval Ball had subsequently to admit that he should be dropped.

My aim was to create controversy. *Dear Sir,* I would write, *I am writing to bring to your attention the deplorable moral standards of the youth of today.* We were in the throes of reaction to war-time immorality and a quiet snog in a shop doorway was the subject for outrage, much of it envious. I would elaborate on this theme until I had expended the requisite number of words to fill the blank space and then sign myself *Disgusted of Goodrington.*

The response to such letters was usually indifferent. Or, to be more precise, non-existent. So the following week I would pen an indignant reply signed *A Teenager.*

It took me some time to appreciate that my letters were misguided. Controversy in a local newspaper has to be local. And many a bright spark from Fleet Street who has become editor of a local rag has gone awry by applying city slickness to parochial issues: the reader wants the lists of mourners and dog-show winners and, however much it might hurt his professional pride, the editor must print them.

When I finally cottoned on I wrote indignant letters about local issues which led to the only occasion when I have fabricated a news story.

The issue was the summer illuminations at Brixham. They were mediocre; nothing more, nothing less. Nevertheless, the subject of raging ferment following the publication in the *Chronicle* of a letter signed *Lamp-Lighter.*

In that letter I castigated those illuminations. By rights the loops of fairy lights, their colours reflected on the sea and pulled into fusions of colour in the harbour waters, should have exploded.

Chewing whatever he chewed, Sellar-Hay said to me: "Good story, laddie, get a follow-up."

It so happened that, at the time, my two greatest friends from school days, Barrie Mullins and Peter Pritchard, were staying with me at my parents' home in Paignton. Ahead of us lay a day of exciting decadence imperilled only by my assignment which was to interview grockels in Brixham and get their views on the illuminations.

I chose my grockels carefully — Barrie Mullins and Peter Pritchard. I interviewed them at length in their bedroom and they duly responded with forthright but utterly conflicting views on the lights extended on the waters of Brixham. To those I added the views of holiday-makers who wished to remain anonymous and in the next edition of the *Chronicle* I had the front-page lead story.

The main problem with creating correspondence, however, was psychological. Before I learned to concentrate on local controversy I ran a grave risk of becoming a certifiable schizophrenic.

It is all very well penning a polemic letter attacking blood sports: it is another matter when, owing to public indifference, you have to subsequently defend what you have lambasted. *"Dear Sir, I was appalled to read the barbaric details of a recent fox-hunt in which hounds in full cry chased their hapless quarry through the grounds of an old folks' home. Needless to say, the emotional shock to these people in the autumn of their lives is incalculable . . . "*

At first my outrage was spurious but, by the time I had reached the kill with the hounds snapping at the exhausted fox, my emotions had become genuine — even if the old folk had leaped from their wheel-chairs with whoops of encouragement.

Unfortunately I failed to arouse either compassionate support or splenetic fury and one week later I was faced with the task of heaping ridicule on my own head.

"Dear Sir, In normal circumstances I would ignore the fatuous and ill-informed views on fox--hunting expressed by your correspondent in these columns last week. But in view of the wide circulation of your estimable newspaper I feel it incumbent upon me to reply. The fact, of course, is that the fox is a pest that must be controlled and the hunt is far more humane than other methods of eradication such as shooting. Perhaps your correspondent would prefer farmers to stalk Reynard with shot-guns thereby leaving him to bleed slowly to death in his lair. The naivety of these do-gooders never fails to astound me . . . "

Take that, Derek Lambert!

The result of these introverted debates was the emergence of a dual personality in company. If someone asked my views on blood sports I would respond with a virulent attack. If the person to whom I was talking was sympathetic he would make his own contribution only to find himself under attack for expressing the self-same views as me. Usually he would wander away in bewilderment and I would observe him later nodding in my direction as he confided to companions that the new young man on the *Chronicle* was as nutty as a fruit-cake.

One week I would be a rabid Socialist; the following week I would emerge as a die-hard Tory. One week a vegetarian, the next a slavering meat-eating freak.

Sometimes the scorn heaped on the head of a correspondent was actionable and readers must have wondered why no libel actions were ever instigated; but, of course, the readers were unaware of the dual roles involved and therefore couldn't comprehend that it would be both masochistic and frivolous to take oneself to the law courts.

* * *

The bleakest periods of my apprenticeship were the times

when I was ejected into the thoroughfares of Dartmouth — Foss Street, Anzac Street, Duke Street, Fairfax Place — with instructions to find a story.

Desperately I prowled the waterfront hoping for some public outrage to be enacted in front of me; wishing pirates onto the yachts moving gently with the currents on the Dart; beckoning sharks in from the open sea; scouring the river shingle for doubloons or World War Two mines. I was never an advocate of violence but, if bombs had to explode somewhere in the world, why not Kingswear railway station?

When any such phenomena failed to materialise I was forced to socialise; to call at the Queen's or the Castle Hotel and invest in a couple of half pints; to chat-up the local tradesmen — Hibbin's stamp shop, the Fairfax sports store, F.J. Prout the hairdresser and tobacconist, Hawke's mobile fish and chip van.

All of which was an ordeal as anyone afflicted with shyness, so often mistaken for diffidence, will understand. In my case my plight was complicated by an extrovert façade which rapidly withered in company. But it was in Dartmouth that any genuine confidence I was to acquire was first established.

In meetings, for instance, with the straw-hatted butchers who dispensed bangers and badinage with equal gusto, their wit as sharp as their bone-slicing blades. As in any small community they were all powerful, domestic serenity in the shape of a tender roast or a meaty pork-chop in their bloodied hands, and with winks, asides, knowing glances and sly innuendo they magnetised the housewives of Dartmouth as surely as Max Miller captivated an audience in a music-hall. Upset the jolly butchers and you were on the way to the divorce courts via stepping-stones of scrag-ends and steaks as tough as a Russian winter.

The police, too, helped to equip me with the verbal

exchanges obligatory to masculine encounters. At first I was merely the stooge on the receiving end of the witticisms reserved for Pressmen, but soon I learned to respond, to attack, with the good-humoured barbs that are aimed at every policeman in the world. When the repartee was established they obliged by doling out a ration of news stories which had hitherto been kept under the counter.

Gradually I learned to adapt my approaches to different citizens. Chameleon-like, I would extract a few items from the clergy at St. Saviour's, piously commending the new stained-glass window, before hurling aside my halo like a discus and exchanging bawdy jokes with members of the darts' league.

Dartmouth also expanded my knowledge of the structures of society. I had grown up in a neat London suburb where life was as ordered as the coming and going of my father who worked in a City bank; I had lived through a war but, evacuation apart, it had hardly touched me — bomb-craters were new playgrounds and shrapnel clattering on the roof was as predictable as summer showers. I had worked briefly in a bank where I was stupefied by the rustle of other people's money. I had served in the RAF where I had vicariously glimpsed other lives through contact with embryonic spivs, miners, gardeners, lawyers, architects and pickpockets, with Scouses, Geordies, Brummies, Taffies, Paddies and Jocks.

But it was Dartmouth that introduced me to the complexities of life because it was a concentrate of endeavour: it had fed upon itself for centuries and it had contained itself within its boundaries, the principal shield being the bridgeless river.

It was a mite incestuous, in places a little mouldy like a neglected hot-house plant cushioned in moss. But beneath the deceptive lassitude of a town becalmed in the countryside, the activities were as industrious, ambitious, passionate and devious as those of any Spanish or Italian town where all is seen and heard.

I learned to peer behind the masks that we all wear. To observe the scars that had moulded men and the bruised sensibilities that had moulded women; to remember the old men, rooted in the riverside gardens, as soldiers bleeding in the mud of the war-to-end-all-wars; to speculate on the erratic fancies of the simpletons dreaming on the slipways. Never to pass judgement on a sly eye or a stiff collar or a cynical mouth. Most importantly I learned to discard much of what I had learned.

And when I caught the last ferry across the river it seemed as if the bows of the *Mew* were severing an artery: the little town, now a cluster of lights bleeding into the water, had been cut adrift from life to lie in a coma until the first ferry of the morning.

Returning to Paignton was like returning to civilisation from the village in Brigadoon. Paignton was hardly Las Vegas but it certainly was civilised in an unimaginative sort of way, planned like a bed of hardy annuals, strictly for holiday-makers; and as such you could not peer in through its windows and observe a microcosm of our society, as you could at Dartmouth.

But I suppose I was prejudiced against Paignton because it was the classroom of my apprenticeship. Shorthand, typing, law and local government, confined to a bungalow in Pines Road overlooking a holiday camp and, in the distance, hills quilted in red and green, coached by my mother and father who must have believed that their parental duties had ended when I was conscripted into the RAF. Without them none of it would have been possible. How could it have been on thirty bob a week?

* * *

59

The finale of the week was, of course, the day before publication. Twelve hours of unrelenting chaos.

The blocks for photographs were missing; the old flat-bed was spitting out nuts and bolts; one of the printers was in a delirium after a night out on scrumpy; there was an acre of space still to be filled.

However dilligently Terry Fleet and I had searched for stories, there was always half a column or so of virgin white newsprint. We extended the column headed STRAY THOUGHTS — items such as "She's the sort of woman one would almost feel disposed to bury for nothing, and do it neatly" (Dickens) — and the week's quotations; we retained a couple of last week's advertisements; we combed council minutes for items of stupefying trivia . . .

One of our standbyes was the poetry supplied by a contributor named Chico from Kingswear. On one occasion the poem wasn't delivered. Another quarter of a column to fill!

I was correcting proofs when Sellar-Hay audibly made his presence known behind me. "How would ye like to turn yon hand to a wee bit of rhyme?"

I swung round in alarm. "I don't know the first thing about poetry."

"Ah well, necessity is the mother of invention."

He left me gazing round the dusty attic in search of inspiration. But not even the sunlight groping through the seagull droppings on the skylight could hatch the muse.

Chico's offerings were always local. What in God's name rhymed with Dartmouth or Brixham? And as for Dart the only word that sprang to mind was fart.

In desperation I scanned the proofs littering the table. Once again Brixham illuminations dominated. Illuminations, lights . . . lights are some sort of cat food . . . so is fish . . . Brixham is synonymous with fish . . .

Desperately I punched out some absurd word-play on lights and handed it to Sellar-Hay who read it, groaned aloud, sat for a full minute with his head in his hands as though seeking Robert Burns' forgiveness, and then subbed it with brutal strokes of his pencil.

By the evening the press was ready to roll or, in the case of the antique flat-bed, to thump. We and the readers were now at the mercy of this temperamental and senile apparatus. A shattered cog, a ruptured pulley and production of the *Chronicle* which had proceeded uninterrupted since 1854 would be halted.

Nellie, as we called the machine, groaned, wheezed, irascibly cast off a couple of spanners left in her innards by the cider-soaked printer and, after a couple of suspenseful moments, ejected the first printed sheet.

Triumphantly we toasted each other in cold, syrup-sweet tea.

The first papers to be printed were copies of the *South Devon Chronicle,* one of the stable of three, which circulated in the villages I covered by bus. This was followed by the *Brixham Chronicle* and finally the Dartmouth edition. But the lack of news was so chronic that there was little to choose between the three papers: the only difference lay in the positioning of the stories. This was a comparatively simple matter: for the *Brixham Chronicle* we would pluck out a Brixham story relegated to the inside pages of the Dartmouth edition and put it on the front page. If you bought both the *Dartmouth* and *Brixham Chronicles* you weren't really getting your money's worth.

It was one evening late in the week when the printers were making these switches that a little old lady with a cherubic face and eyes as blue and clear as a baby's came into the office. I spoke to her at a safe distance from the flat-bed which was liable to caterpault its parts at lethal velocities when under stress.

"Yes, madam," I said, "and what can I do for you?"

"How's your nose for news?" she asked, her voice crisp and bright with a hint of North Country in it.

"Fair to middling," I said.

"It should be twitching, young man."

"Why's that, madam?"

"Because I've got a story for you, young man."

I waited expectantly but she seemed reluctant to elaborate.

"Perhaps you could give me some details . . . "

"I want you to come with me," she said. "Get the story first-hand. Don't rely on the word of an old woman like me."

"But I must know — "

"Do you want a scoop or don't you?" she demanded.

I went upstairs to consult Sellar-Hay. "Is she aw right in the head?" he asked.

"She seems sane enough."

He stared at me as though doubting whether I was qualified to express an opinion. "It's up to ye, laddie," he said finally. "Ye've got to make your own judgement some day."

The old lady had a black Ford Popular waiting outside. Inside were three cats and piles of cat-smelling blankets and cushions. "That's Cuddles, Tiger and Napoleon," she said. "If they like you they'll purr."

Silence.

She started the car in gear; we jerked forward and stopped. "These modern cars," she said.

We headed towards Townstal, the council estate overlooking the town. It was a wild evening with a wind sweeping in from the sea and clouds flying low in the sky. If the wind reached Force 8 and the tide was right it was not unknown for the car ferry to be swept out to sea; I could imagine Sellar-Hay's reaction if I missed the story for the Dartmouth edition.

"Well," I said conversationally as we narrowly missed a cyclist, "perhaps you can tell me what it's all about now?"

She took a bend on the wrong side of the road. "You've got to hear it for yourself," she said.

"Hear it?"

She chuckled. "Rudolph could be the making of you, young man."

"Who," I asked, "is Rudolph?"

"You'll see."

I made a wild guess. "Is he a dog?" There had been a dog on television that supposedly answered questions, and Noel Whitcomb, the chirpy *Daily Mirror* columnist, was writing about a talking dog at that time.

"You'll see," she said.

"Incidentally," I said, with a sudden premonition that we were heading for Land's End, "where are we going?"

"We're here," she said as the car skidded to a halt outside a thatched cottage.

She rang the doorbell while we waited, the old lady, Cuddles, Tiger, Napoleon and me.

After a couple of minutes we heard a scratching on the other side of the door. Was this Rudolph? A slavering beast with two heads? The wind whined through the thatch.

The door creaked open to reveal another old lady whose head bobbed up and down as she peered out. "Who's that?" she asked suspiciously.

"It's the young man from the *Chronicle* and he's come to hear Rudolph."

The second old lady's head bobbed. "Lot of darned nonsense," she said.

We went into the lounge where the smell of cats was overpowering. There were cats on the sofa, cats behind the curtains, cats on the chairs; wherever you looked there was feline life and eyes glowed in dim corners.

The second old lady cleared a cat off an armchair, sat down and said: "I told you not to tell anyone about Rudolph."

"Stop bullying me," said the first old lady.

"And taking my car as well," said the second old lady.

I had a momentary vision of Old Lady No. 2 sitting at the controls, head bobbing behind the wheel. "Do you mean to say that wasn't your car?" I said sternly to Old Lady No. 1.

"She hasn't even got a licence," said Old Lady No. 2.

"Don't need one."

"Oh yes you do."

"Don't."

"I wonder," I interrupted, "whether I could hear Rudolph."

"Of course," said Old Lady No. 1 with a charming smile.

She went into another room and the second old lady said: "Don't take any notice of her, she's barmy."

The first old lady returned with a box in which, I assumed, Rudolph resided.

"Now you just listen," said the first old lady.

She opened the box and the wizened head of a tortoise popped out. "Listen," she said. "Just listen."

I stared at the tortoise which stared back from dusty eyes.

"Go on, young man, speak to him."

What did you say to a tortoise? *Good day to you, sir, nasty weather we're having.* I said: "Hallo."

The tortoise looked very wise in that room at that moment. Then it withdrew inside its shell.

"Did you hear it?" the first old lady demanded.

"I'm afraid I didn't," I said.

"Then you're deaf. You should go to the doctor. What's the good of being a reporter if you can't hear properly?"

I looked appealingly at the second old lady who touched her head significantly. She added: "I told her the sod wouldn't speak today — he's got a cold."

I smiled, backing away through furry bodies entwining themselves between my legs. I opened the door, I bowed, I was gone.

I walked back thoughtfully through the rain. It was my first experience with an occupational hazard of the profession: an encounter with some of those readers who are euphemistically described as eccentrics.

Half an hour later I stood dripping in front of Sellar-Hay. He looked up. "Well?"

"Nothing in it," I said.

"Be more precise, laddie."

"She wasn't quite right in the head."

"What did she want?"

"Well," I said hopelessly, "she had a tortoise and she thought it talked."

He stared at me thoughtfully. I guessed his mind had returned to the hat-sniffing episode. "Aye," he said after a long pause, "well, you may be interested to know that while you've been long gone the car ferry's been swept oot to sea."

VI

Many of the drunks who appeared in the dock at Dartmouth Magistrates Court had tippled with the West Country brew called scrumpy.

Scrumpy is a rough cider which owes its popularity to its cheapness — about sixpence a pint in those days — and its potency. Its alcoholic content isn't high and yet two pints is sufficient to dispatch the uninitiated howling legless into the night. It tastes like vinegar and has as many addicts in Devon as marijuana at a pop concert.

Having seen its gibbering victims looking as if they had just escaped from Broadmoor, I should have known better. But, after a depressing week of funerals and munching reproach from Sellar-Hay, I agreed to go for a couple of pints with Arthur, the red-faced printer — and on thirty shillings a week those pints had to be scrumpy.

Not every pub sold scrumpy because the landlords objected to addicts and unwary holiday-makers wrecking their premises before collapsing in untidy heaps on the pavement outside; so we headed for a public bar in the back streets, picking up the first whiff of rotten apples fifty yards away.

The bar was like all the other scrumpy haunts. Yellow walls, ceiling stained brown with tobacco smoke, basic furniture too heavy to be picked up and thrown through the window, a bar bereft of any accessories and a barman capable of taking care of himself.

We ordered two half pints and assessed the scene.

In one corner two men were squaring up to each other without having taken the precaution of standing up; with loosely-bunched fists they swung harmless punches like kittens pawing the air before rain. Another sat with his head on his arms uttering small, bubbling snores.

Alone and assured sat a woman in late middle-age sipping a half pint of the lethal beverage. Her hair was blonde and black-rooted; fingernails lacquered with peeling varnish; cheeks rouged like a Russian doll's, but her glory was her eyelashes which had been curled and cultivated and fluttered like two palms in a desert.

Her aplomb was magnificent. She sipped her scrumpy as though it were a Martini cocktail; she surveyed the dazed men around her as though they were young gallants lusting after her body; she flicked cigarette ash from her skirt as though she held a silken fan in her hand.

Arthur sipped his scrumpy and said: "How do you fancy that?"

"I don't," I said.

Arthur looked aggrieved: youth slighting the desires of the middle-aged. And I suppose it was then that he decided to get me drunk.

He ordered three more halves, carrying one over to the woman with the eyelashes.

"Charmed I'm sure," she said.

"My pleasure," said Arthur.

She took out a Woodbine from a packet of five and waited patiently while Arthur, like a waiter anticipating a handsome tip, fumbled with his matches. When he had lit the cigarette she dismissed him with a nod of her head.

"Goes like a rattlesnake," Arthur confided.

"Looks like one," I said. "Do you know her?"

"I've seen her around."

"Then how do you know . . ?"

"She gave me the wink," replied Arthur in the manner of all rebuffed males.

We drank our second halves which didn't taste quite as bad as the first. There was no apparent effect, merely an exaggerated awareness that I was totally, utterly, indisputably, coldstone sober.

"She'd go for you," Arthur remarked. "You being a reporter," a nibble of sarcasm in his voice.

"I should be so lucky," I said, words perfectly enunciated.

In the corner one of the two sedentary pugilists took a wild swipe at his opponent, missed and slid to the floor. The barman picked him up, dumped him outside and went on polishing glasses.

In came two holiday-makers, fresh-faced North Countrymen, and ordered two pints.

The barman said: "You'm drunk this stuff before?"

They grinned at each other: they were talking to a local yokel. "Weaned on Newcastle Brown," said one. "Doest think a drop of apple-juice could hurt us?"

The barman shrugged and poured two pints. The woman with the eyelashes belched and patted her smudged lips with a wisp of soiled handkerchief.

"Down the hatch," said one of the new customers.

"Mud in your eye," said the other.

They poured the two pints down their throats without swallowing and ordered two more. The barman, as phlegmatic as a Hollywood butler, poured them. The bar smelled like a neglected orchard.

"One for the road?" asked Arthur.

"Of course."

The occupants of the bar had come into clear focus. I saw them all as teenagers and concocted stories about their lives, literary genius surfacing from fermented apple juice.

The fourth half — and the fifth — slipped down my throat like oil. I mourned for these people navigated to this bar by the injustices of life.

At this juncture one of the North Countrymen detached himself from the bar and turned in the direction of the toilet. He looked as though he were walking through quick-sand; long, slow-motion strides as his knees bent beneath him; finally he lay face-down on the floor.

His friend said defensively to the barman: "He supped a few before he came here, you know."

The barman shrugged and began to read the *Herald Express*.

The second North Countryman went after his companion. He moved faster but his knees also betrayed him and he lay down and fell asleep beside his friend.

The barman finished reading an article about Torquay United before grasping each of them by the shoulders and pulling them out into the street. Then he telephoned the police station from the bar. "Three outside," he said. Then: "'Tis up to you. Probably two or three more before night's out."

It was at this juncture that the woman with the eyelashes winked at me. A languorous, theatrical wink with one fern-like lash.

I smiled at her. She must have looked like Rita Hayworth in her day. In fact she wasn't unattractive now. "Would you like a drink?" I asked.

"A gin please, dear."

"Aye, aye," said Arthur.

She poured the gin into her scrumpy and took two sips which emptied half the glass. The long lash flickered again. "Nothing like a drop of Mother's Ruin," she remarked, her accent as Cockney as a Pearly Queen's.

I winked back.

"Thought she looked like a rattlesnake," whispered Arthur.

I ignored him. Her past unfolded before me. One of a family of thirteen, father on the booze, mother on the game, forced out to work at the age of twelve, straight into service, bettering herself all the time, seduced by a footman, nearly dying in childbirth, battling on against the odds, finally marrying an honest young man who enlisted for King and country in 1939 and was killed at Dunkirk. And yet here she was, still arrogantly defying cruel fate, the Duchess of the Scrumpy Bar.

"One for the road?" I said to Arthur.

He held onto the bar, face flaming brighter than ever. "Why not?" He righted the swaying bar. "Why bloody not?"

"Last orders," said the barman.

Arthur said: "Tenminishtogoyet."

The barman produced an old-fashioned policeman's truncheon and placed it on the bar. "Last orders," he repeated.

And there I was still sober. Creative impulses jostling each other, vision unimpaired, speech as precise as a drill sergeant's.

"Another little drop?" the Duchess asked, fluttering both lashes.

"Of course. Why not champagne?"

"Shteady on," muttered Arthur.

The barman poured her a gin. "You've got one minute to drink it," he said, folding the *Herald Express* and stuffing it into his pocket.

I finished my scrumpy in one swallow. Arthur dropped his glass and the barman said: "That'll cost you." The Duchess downed her cocktail with a couple more sips.

"And now you can all bugger off," the barman remarked picking up his truncheon.

The sleeping drunks awoke as though an alarm clock had

sounded and walked with unfaltering steps to the door. The Duchess and myself followed with Arthur bringing up the rear, cannoning off tables and chairs.

Outside, the police were shovelling up a couple of customers.

One of the policemen recognised me and said: "Hallo, scribe, what the hell be you'm doing in there."

"Seeking life's rich pageantry," I told him. Perhaps there was a story in the Duchess. A feature, a novel. I decided with innate chivalry to see her home.

Arthur was waltzing away in the direction of the ferry.

"Better get home, scribe," said the policeman," or else you'll be reporting your own rich pageantry in the dock tomorrow."

I stared at him outraged. But, as I searched my mind for a suitably cutting reply, the shock-waves of fresh-air hit me.

"Ossifer . . . "

The Duchess took my arm. "Best do as he says, ducks."

But my legs wouldn't move. Someone had filled my shoes with lead. The stars chased each other around the sky. I heard the whoosh of a train entering a tunnel, the sound of waves on a pebble shore.

"Come on, dearie. Don't want to spend the night in the nick, now do we?"

And now my feet were weightless, prancing ahead of me. I could leap canyons, vault castles.

"Steady on," said the Duchess. "You nearly fell in the gutter that time."

I wanted to tell her that soon she would be famous. Rags to riches. The story of a street urchin spanning two tumultuous decades of the twentieth century.

"Better hurry, dear," she said, "the last ferry goes in a minute."

A wooden ramp led from the street down a covered passage to the ferry which was boarded by a gangway. Before every crossing passengers would pound down the wooden boards only to see the gangway whisked away by a triumphant member of the crew.

At the top of the ramp I sensed that the crewman was waiting for me, timing the removal of the gangway to the last second. The Duchess began to run down the incline pulling me behind her. At the bottom I stumbled and fell into her arms.

And that was how we stood, locked in a fierce embrace, like soldier and sweetheart parting in war-time, when, through scrumpy-crazed eyes, I noticed Maureen, the girl on the train, staring at me from the rails of the ferry.

The crewman in charge of the gangway must have been in a peculiarly benevolent frame of mind because he let me on. But Maureen had disappeared.

Arthur and myself lapsed into unconsciousness on the train, waking at Newton Abbot where we spent the rest of the night in the waiting room.

Maureen was indulgently forgiving next morning but our relationship was never quite the same.

I saw the Duchess only once more — in the dock at Torquay police court accused of soliciting sailors on the Strand.

Several weeks later my mother, emptying the pockets of my sports coat before taking it to the cleaners, held up a small, dark object and said: "What on earth is this, dear?"

From a distance it looked like a dead spider. On closer inspection it proved to be a false black eyelash.

VII

Season of mists and mellow fruitfulness.

September was fusing into October; the air smelled of bonfires, the trees were tapestries of amber light, the lazy summer throb of the fishing boats at sea had been sharpened by the first frost.

The holiday-makers had gone home and the resorts of Torbay and the South Hams were taking stock like the towns and villages of France after the German occupation had started.

For this is really *their* time. Summer is the working day, feeding and entertaining the city folk: autumn is the evening. Once again regulars occupy their rightful seats in the pub, once again the landladies linger in the shops to swop tales of grockels' perfidy.

Fairy lights are extinguished, flowerbeds of salvias and petunias lie fallow, waves toss spray over the promenade. In the parks solitary men walk their dogs around deserted bandstands and the cries of children are shrill and sad on the cold air.

But this is not a time of hibernation. Locals resume activities abandoned during the summer recess: the local operatic society is casting *The Mikado,* the Chess Club is searching for lost pawns, historians, naturalists and archaeologists are rooting around the countryside in search of specimens, at Black Awton nudist colony they are counting their goose pimples.

Nor is this a time of repose for Pressmen.

National newspapers rely largely on the ranks of local correspondents to supply them with news. Freelances and Press agencies apart, these correspondents are mostly local newspapermen.

Competition is frequently bitter especially in South Devon with Christmas approaching. By this time Sellar-Hay had sufficient faith in me to allow me to use his name to phone stories to the nationals — he took half the proceeds — and I had become Dartmouth stringer for the *Western Morning News,* an elegant daily not unlike the *Daily Telegraph,* published in Plymouth, and the *Torbay Herald Express,* an evening paper with one of the best lay-outs in provincial journalism.

Lineage, as the system is known, worked well enough for me in Dartmouth. Not so in the fringe areas, the no man's-land, where vendettas were conducted with gangland ferocity.

Brixham brought out the worst in us. A police court case with obvious potential for the nationals would finish and another would begin. With exaggerated nonchalance a reporter would stretch, put down his pencil and murmur: "Fill in for me would you, old man, I feel like a cup of coffee."

Once outside the courthouse he became a man possessed. Rushing across the road to the telephone box, impatiently making transfer-charge calls to Fleet Street numbers and rattling off the story direct from his notes.

But the cards were stacked against me in Brixham. In the first place I had to stay in court to record a bicycle without lights or a motorist without a licence; in the second place there was little point in dictating a story direct from my notes because it took me most of the afternoon to decipher them.

Whenever I did get through to Fleet Street a bored voice would say: "Sorry, old man, we've just had that from Page of Torquay." Which was fair enough because I had no justifiable claim on Brixham lineage.

* * *

My big lineage scoop occurred after a day at Brixham police court.

I looked forward to Brixham because the court didn't begin until 10.30 am and I could linger in bed before catching a bus from Paignton; also there was a fair chance that I would meet some of the reporters from the local daily papers. Johnny Dudman of the *Herald Express* who later took himself to Fleet Street, Roy Page of the *Western Morning News*, bespectacled and assured with his story written before the court concluded, Irene Leonard also of the *Morning News*. She was a smart little girl from the north who wore dazzling clothes which mesmerised many an official into delivering a good quote; she was also kind-hearted enough to accompany me to the cinema and pub and go Dutch as I searched the pockets of my sports jacket for small change. When I was last in Torquay she was still on the *Morning News*, still dazzling them in council chamber and courtroom.

After Brixham court that day I took the bus to Kingswear. As the bus sped past green cushions of land scattered with red-leafed thickets, the embers of summer, I brooded about my contributions to the National Press. I so far had managed only a few paragraphs and I yearned for a banner headline slapped across six columns.

I caught the ferry to Dartmouth and was on my way to the office to tackle my notes when I met a friendly doctor emerging from the Castle Hotel. We walked round the boatfloat together while I harassed him with questions. I thirsted for news as an alcoholic thirsts for liquor, and almost everything was news of a sort — you could sell an item about fertiliser to *Farmers' Weekly*, a piece about street traders to *World's Fair*, a couple of paragraphs about a drunken holiday-maker to his local paper.

We were starting our second circuit of the float when the doctor said casually: "I hear they've got a case of smallpox in the hospital."

I stopped. The doctor said: "I suppose that's news ... "

"That's news," I said, inspecting him closely to determine how much wine he had consumed with his lunch.

"Well there you are," he said soberly, "you've got a story."

"Who's got smallpox?"

"A seaman, I gather. He was put ashore last night."

"Are you sure?"

"That's what I was told. Don't quote me, but ... " This is one of the most frequent expressions used in the presence of the Press and often precedes a stream of outrageous gossip. In this case it was merely hearsay information.

"Thank you, doctor," I muttered. I wandered away in a daze, day-dreaming of headlines. SMALLPOX SCARE. VACCINE RUSHED TO PLAGUE PORT. EMERGENCY DEBATE ON SMALLPOX OUTBREAK. I had been handed a scoop. In the taverns of Fleet Street they would remember it as they still remembered Arthur Christiensen's airship scoop.

But what to do with it? This is the continual dilemma of the freelance. You can give it to one newspaper and earn a fat bonus but, at the same time, earn the undying displeasure of all the other papers. Or you can distribute it to everyone.

I walked up and down the waterfront. Journalism, they say, is ninety per cent luck and ten per cent knowing what to do with it. The beneficent gods had ladled out their ninety per cent, the balance was up to me.

First of all, was it true? At this stage in my career I had become canny: if I checked with the hospital authorities they might issue an official statement or tip off a freelance and my story would be as exclusive as a fish and chip supper.

Just then I spotted a male nurse from the hospital whom I knew vaguely. I asked him about the smallpox.

"It's true enough. Getting ready to whip him off to an isolation hospital."

I asked him to find out the name, age and nationality of the patient and he agreed to do this for five shillings, a fraction of what I would earn from the scoop.

Armed with the details I returned to the office to find that Sellar-Hay was in Torquay, Terry Fleet was touring the villages and the office manager had taken the afternoon off. At 5 pm the printers all went home; I was alone, I was in charge.

I typed out differently worded stories for the various newspapers. Then, with shaking hand, I picked up the earpiece of the antique telephone and, speaking into the mouthpiece on the desk as though I were broadcasting, I asked for a transfer charge call to one of the Fleet Street papers.

The operator asked a switchboard operator if he would accept a call from Mr Sellar-Hay of Dartmouth. He said he would. "Copy, please," I said lighting a cigarette and pushing an imaginary hat onto the back of my head.

"Sellar-Hay of Dartmouth," I said to the copy-taker; in the background I could hear the clatter of typewriters.

"Who?"

"Sellar-Hay, Dartmouth."

"How do you spell that, old man?"

I spelled it. Now there are several varieties of copy-takers, each of them an expert typist, each recognising a good story and a bad one with the same instinct as a news editor. There is the bored copy-taker who, half way through your dictation, asks: "Is there much more of this, old man?" There is the comedian who lapses into helpless laughter when you make some point of momentous import. There is the pedant who knows the newspaper's style better than you and corrects you as you stumble along. There is the speed merchant who sighs: "I'm waiting, old boy," while you wrestle with a shorthand outline.

My copy-taker was the pedant.

"Ready when you are," he said after we'd sorted out the spelling of Sellar-Hay.

Now there arose a problem. With admirable loyalty I was putting over the story in Sellar-Hay's name. Just the same I wanted a slice of the cake; it *was* my exclusive. "Underneath," I said, "could you put *On Information Supplied by Derek Lambert.*"

The typewriter clattered at breakneck speed. A pause. "Is that the intro, old boy?"

"Is that the what?"

"Is that the first paragraph? Doesn't seem to make sense."

"No," I said. Then: "Wait a minute," noticing that I had set fire to my notes with my cigarette. Frantically I beat out the flames with a brochure advertising boat trips up the Dart.

When I picked up the earpiece and mouthpiece again he was saying plaintively: "Are you still there, old man?"

"Yes, now about that sentence. It's not actually part of the story. I just wanted to make sure that you realised that the tip came from Derek Lambert."

"Ah." Another pause. "Are you Sellar-Hay or Derek Lambert?"

"Well, actually I'm Derek Lambert."

"But you said — "

"I'm Sellar-Hay's deputy. I didn't want to confuse you."

Another sigh as though an ulcer was nagging him. Then: "With respect, old man, I shouldn't like to be around when you were actually trying to confuse me."

I heard him rip out the paper and start again.

Together we navigated the first paragraph. Then I went on: "The victim is — "

"Not victim, old man."

"Why?"

"*We* don't like victim. Not unless he's dead that is. Is he dead?"

"No, he's not dead." At least I hoped he wasn't.

"What about *the patient?*"

I considered this. It seemed to lack dramatic impact. "The sick man is — " the shrug of his shoulders reached me through the receiver — "a Lascar."

"What's that, old man?"

"A Lascar."

"Alaska?"

"No," I shouted, "A LASCAR. A LASCAR SEAMAN."

"Ah, a Lascar. No need to shout, old man."

It had never been like this with James Cagney. I put my feet on the desk and the chair crashed backwards taking me with it. At first I thought I had broken my neck. Faintly I could hear his voice: "Are you there, old man?"

When I regained my seat and the receiver I heard him telling one of his colleagues: "It's all right for you, mate, but I've got a nutter on the end of my line."

I went on: "An emergency dash — "

He groaned. I asked him: "Anything wrong with that?"

"Nothing wrong with it, old man."

"Then why are you groaning?"

"Bit of a cliche, isn't it?"

"I like it," I said. "It's *my* cliche and I love it."

"Okay, old man, keep your shirt on."

After I had finished dictating the story that would be emblazoned across the front page of the paper he asked: "What's the weather like down there."

"Fair to middling," I said.

"Pissing down up here," he said and cut me off.

It took me an hour to dictate all the stories; then I sat back and waited for the phone to ring. It did, endlessly. *News Chronicle, Daily Express, Mail, Mirror, Sketch, Telegraph* . . . Normally they would have dispatched staffmen from Plymouth, but the staffmen were in Cornwall on a murder so it was all down to Sellar-Hay. They wanted more details, anything I could give them. They had also contacted the health authorities, they said, but couldn't get any response. But Sellar-Hay was a respected journalist: they accepted his story.

I caught the last ferry and the last train; as I left the office the phone was still ringing.

I went to bed with emotions that, from time to time, assail every daily journalist — exhilaration that gradually subsides into exhausted satisfaction, sleep delayed by anticipation of the morning's papers.

I was on my way to the railway station before Joe had even blown a kiss to his motorbike. On the platform I tried to see the headlines but they were hidden by wrapping paper; finally the sleepy attendant at the kiosk cut the string with a pocket knife and I leaped at him. I bought every morning paper and sat down to scan the front pages.

And there it was on the front pages. Not splashed across the whole page but by God it filled a few column inches, and in one paper it was spread across four columns.

Maureen wasn't on the train that morning. But the printer was duly impressed and I heard other passengers discussing the smallpox outbreak. *My* smallpox outbreak!

On my way past the boat-float to the office I met the doctor who had given me the tip.

"Seen the papers?" I asked.

He looked tired. "Not yet." He yawned. "By the way, that smallpox I was telling you about. It turned out to be chicken-pox."

* * *

Sellar-Hay's anger was spectacular; if we hadn't got smallpox, I thought, at least we would have a coronary.

He chewed terribly. He punched the palms of his hands with his fists. He used strange oaths full of rolling "r's" and phlegm-filled gutterals. "To think ye used ma bluidy name," he moaned. "Made a bluidy fool o' me, you Sassenach half-wit."

I bore the abuse with dignity. If I had tried to speak I might have burst into tears.

"Na get oot o' my sight for ever. You're sacked. You're fired. A reporter? A bluidy hotel porter more like. Now get oot," his voice cracking with fury.

I went back to Paignton. For most of the day I sat on the golf-course overlooking Torbay as the rain swept in from the sea. The date was October 10th, 1950, and at 7.30 pm I went home to celebrate my twenty-first birthday.

VIII

With two pounds borrowed from my father — I didn't reveal
to my parents that I had been sacked until years later — I
employed a secretarial agency to type twenty-five identical letters to daily and evening newspapers all over Britain.

How could any editor refuse my services? According to the
letter I had served with distinction in the RAF; I was proficient
in shorthand and typing; I was ready to travel anywhere, dedicated to justice and accuracy; I was a student of law, local government and typography. In brief I was a pillar of journalistic
rectitude — and a palpable liar.

None of the editors or their assistants who daily receive
sheafs of similar letters was fooled. But the editor of the *Eastern
Daily Press* and *Evening News,* published in Norwich, did grant
me an interview in their Fleet Street offices.

Fleet Street! At last I was there. Brushing shoulders with
famous scribes, peering into the beery-breathed mouths of journalists' pubs — the Falstaff, the Kings and Keys, the Punch,
Mooneys, the Bell — gawping at the shining black offices of
the *Daily Express* and the dignified portals of the *Daily Telegraph.*

With hands deep in the pockets of my raincoat, collar firmly
up, I strode purposefully down The Street hoping that the
pretty secretaries abroad for their lunch-time break would
assume I was a crime reporter intent upon some stunning exposure — Duncan Webb, perhaps, of *The People* who exposed the

Messina brothers.

From the exits of the *Evening News, Evening Standard* and *Star* scuttled old-fashioned vans stacked with bundles of newspapers which were hurled onto the pavement and slapped onto news-stands. "Late Extra. Body found on Clapham Common. Read all about it."

I was drunk with it.

Besotted.

And full of myself when I presented myself to the editor of the *Eastern Daily Press,* an austere, likeable man with a glimmer of humour in his eyes.

He interrogated me with terrifying logic.

"Why did you always want to work for the *Eastern Daily Press?*"

"Because I've always regarded it as a fine example of its type."

"And what is that, Mr. Lambert?"

What indeed!

"A respectable — "

"Rag?"

"No, sir," indignantly.

"What then?"

Inspiration. "A sort of *Times,* sir."

"You're sure you're not referring to the *East Anglian Daily Times?*" — a rival publication in that neck of the woods.

"No, sir, the *Eastern Daily Press.*"

"Known as the EDP."

"So I believe . . . "

"But why choose the EDP, Mr. Lambert? After all, it's a long way from your home." A pause while he picked up my letter and scanned it. "You imply that you've selected the *Eastern Daily Press* out of all the provincial daily newspapers as the best medium for your talents . . . "

"I didn't mean to appear conceited, sir."

"Not a bad thing, Mr. Lambert. Not a bad thing at all. Conceit?" He shrugged. "At least you have ambition. Would you stay with us if I offered you a job?"

A tricky one this. "To be honest, sir, I suppose that if I were offered a position on a national newspaper in the years to come I would accept it."

Pompous ass!

"At least you're honest, Mr. Lambert."

"Thank you, sir."

"And you really mean to tell me that out of all the provincial daily papers you have chosen the *Eastern Daily Press* as the next stepping stone after the ... ah ... *Dartmouth Chronicle?*"

I looked him straight in the eyes and said I had.

"Strange," he said. "Because there were two letters in your envelope. Both had identical wording. One was addressed to the *Eastern Daily Press,* the other to the *Manchester Guardian.*"

He burst out laughing.

I got the job.

* * *

I was sent to the King's Lynn office of the *Eastern Daily Press* and *Evening News* — two separate papers. King's Lynn lies to the north-west of Norfolk near the mouth of the Great Ouse which pours its muddy waters into The Wash where — as I never tired of recalling in feature stories — King John was reputed to have lost his jewels.

It had some fine old architecture — steeped in history — but it seemed to me to be an unattractive town, a contradiction of its regal name. Apart from a fine wide square it consisted of two main shopping streets of nondescript stores and an expanse of soggy parkland surrounded by terraces of houses.

But, to be fair, it didn't have much going for it in the winter. The town itself was bordered on one side by fields of sugar-beet and on the other by the grey-brown river. Its dominant industry — fleecing American servicemen apart — was processing the sugar-beet, and the factory emitted a sweet sticky odour which I can smell to this day.

King's Lynn's natural handicaps were compounded by its foreign population — American servicemen, American servicemen's camp followers, itinerant labour for the sugar-beet crop and Z reservists called up for refresher courses in the arts of war.

These various contingents met after closing-time on a Saturday night and beat the bejesus out of each other, the usual targets for unprovoked attack being the Americans because, as in the war, they still had pots of money, sharp uniforms, crew-cuts, Hollywood voices and, of course, they got the girls. *Utility knickers — one Yank and they're down,* as the war-time joke went.

Not that anyone envied them some of the girls who hitch-hiked across the British Isles to be near the American bases. The girls set up bawdy houses, bought well-sprung caravans, took to the flooded sugar-beet fields or operated in shop doorways in the High Street, thus affording the local constabulary many a satisfactory pinch.

But it was all pretty squalid.

And depressing when I first viewed it, wearing my raincoat, my only suit — double-breasted, worsted, with a faint pink stripe, a twenty-first birthday present — and carrying a cardboard suitcase held together by a frayed leather strap that had been used by my father in World War One.

I made my way from the railway station to the first of the many lodging houses I was to inhabit during my spell in King's Lynn. During this interlude in my life I became an authority on lodging houses, their owners and occupants.

The first was managed by a plump lady and her husband who was a train driver. It was cheap and comfortable occupied by Paul, a handsome and raffish commercial traveller who wore elegant suits, suede shoes and a tie which seemed to have been spun from gold, the manager of Liptons, and myself. But accommodation was only available for a few weeks.

My next nesting place was theatrical. There was only one theatre in King's Lynn but music hall was still popular, and the evening meal was always an exciting prospect because you might share it with a slick, shiny-haired juggler who would dexterously manipulate the boiled spuds; a comedian trying out his gags over the college pudding; a ventriloquist who made voices emerge from the cod fillet; or doll-like soubrettes who squeaked and giggled their way through the Windsor soup. What we really needed was an illusionist who could make the food edible.

After injudiciously complaining about the meals I was given a week's notice and I moved to a modern semi-detached owned by a widow in her mid-thirties, a change which proved to be even more injudicious than the complaint about the food.

She was plump, flushed, excessively house-proud and talked about her late husband as though he were still alive. (He had died from a heart-attack in mysterious circumstances.)

"I think we're going to be friends," she said on the first evening as we sat in the living room — a room, in fact, that was never lived-in and looked like a tableau to be exhibited in a museum one hundred years from now as an example of a suburban dwelling in the nineteen-fifties.

The floral curtains hung in undisturbed folds; imitation-leather easy chairs and sofa were grouped round an electric fire equipped with simulated coal; on the mantelpiece stood a wedding photograph of my landlady and her bridegroom, toothy and Brylcreemed, little resembling "the lion of a man" whose exploits were often recounted to me; in the bookshelves were *The Encyclopaedia Britannica* and *The Complete Works of Charles Dickens*.

I immediately dropped cigarette ash on the hearth-rug. She stared at it for a moment before rushing into the kitchen, as though the stew had boiled over, and returning with dustpan and brush.

"I see we must get more ashtrays," she remarked. "I hope you don't smoke in bed."

"Only when I'm very hot," I said.

She looked at me strangely, the way Sellar-Hay sometimes regarded me. "Wilfred has never smoked," she said.

"Wilfred?"

"My husband. He doesn't drink either," she went on. "Except for a little ginger wine at Christmas. Do you drink?"

"An occasional beer," I confessed.

She shook her head sadly. "Dinner's always at six-thirty sharp."

"I'm afraid I shall be late sometimes. You know, we work odd hours."

"Then perhaps you'll be good enough to telephone me. I'm always at home. In fact, since Wilfred — "

"I'll telephone you," I said.

It was after the first week that she began communicating with me through the dog. This, it transpired, was a method of expressing displeasure at some misdemeanour. Displeasure was expressed in a sliding scale of reproof: total outrage was projected through notes pinned up at the scene of the crime and this was preferable to the use of the dog as an intermediary because at least I knew what I had done.

The notes written in capital letters appeared all over the house. PLEASE PULL THE CHAIN AFTER USE. And beside my bowl of

tinned grapefruit one morning: GENTLEMEN SHAVE BEFORE
BREAKFAST.

The dog, a moth-eaten poodle with knowing eyes, was
employed on the subjects of smoking, drinking and sex,
although sex was never actually named.

Pepi was the little brute's name and he would sit, head swi-
velling from mistress to recalcitrant, as she confided to him:
"Wilfred isn't a smoker," as though he were sitting on the
other side of the kitchen table. "He knows it's bad for the
health."

Much good it did him, I thought.

"And even if he did he would never leave a cigarette end in
the soap dish."

Or: "I've never once smelled alcohol on Wilfred's breath,
have you, Pepi?"

Pepi's bright eyes stared at me accusingly.

"I think someone had difficulty in negotiating the stairs last
night, don't you, Pepi?"

A canine nod.

"Dreadful places public houses. So common."

I poured myself my second cup of tea — my allowance —
reflecting bitterly that I had only been able to afford two
halves of bitter the previous evening and, accompanied by a
waitress from a coffee shop in the High Street, had finally been
ejected from the pub because I was bad for business.

"The trouble with alcohol, Pepi, is that it makes men reck-
less."

Great Jehosophat! What was coming now?

Pepi licked his lips.

"And it makes them sly. They lurk in the bushes as far away
as possible from the street lights."

She must have had the eyesight of a night-fighter pilot
because I had kissed the waitress goodnight a hundred yards

down the road; a fluttering perfunctory sort of kiss — any cavalier intentions had been deflated by ejection from the pub.

I have subsequently wondered why I stayed at the widow's digs. Because, I suppose, it was cheap, the food was good, it was handy for the office and NO VACANCY signs hung everywhere else in the town.

I stayed there for four months until the denouement one frosty winter morning.

I awoke as usual curled in the foetal position seeking the warmth of the womb. There were frost patterns *inside* the windows — glacial flowers, rushes and stars — and my nose was as cold and wet as a dog's.

But, perversely, I enjoyed this room: it was a sanctuary, a haven for my material possessions and private thoughts. When I turned over, the bed made noises as though there was a deranged double-bass player hiding underneath; the floorboards were covered with chipped linoleum; the taps in the washbasin shuddered feverishly when turned on. The washbasin had always been fertile ground for written reprimands. IF YOU CLOSE YOUR MOUTH WHILST CLEANING TEETH YOU WILL NOT SPRAY TOOTHPASTE ON THE MIRROR. And PLEASE DRAW CURTAINS DURING ABLUTIONS AS THERE HAVE BEEN COMPLAINTS FROM NEIGHBOURS.

I looked at my watch. 7.30 am. Time for the early morning cup of tea. As usual there was a knock on the door, the clink of cup against saucer. But this time the knock was more peremptory than usual. "Do you mind if I come in?"

Good God, what had I done? Had a dog-end dropped down the washbasin plughole and found its way down the drainpipe? Was there mud on the stair carpet? Had a neighbour once again spotted me in my RAF pants and vest?

She came in and stood at my bedside while I propped myself up on the pillows. She was wearing a red dressing-gown and

89

she smelled of perfume; her hair had been fluffed out and she had applied a little lipstick.

I eyed her warily.

"I thought I'd bring it into you so's you don't have to get out in the cold."

"That's very kind of you," I said.

"It seems sort of lonely in here."

"I'm quite happy," I said.

"And cold. Would you like a hot-water bottle these cold nights?"

"That would be nice," I said.

"Of course you don't feel the cold when you're married."

I smiled at her uncertainly.

"I brought you a biscuit with your tea. A digestive. Do you like them?"

"My favourites," I told her.

She leaned over the bed to hand me my tea and digestive biscuit, at which point her dressing-gown fell open revealing that she wore nothing underneath.

I moved to the other side of the bed, but two hanging bosoms followed me. "No," she suddenly shouted, "you mustn't, you mustn't, it's not right."

I dropped the teacup and saucer on the linoleum.

She was breathing like a marathon runner nearing the winning post and sobbing: "Please respect me. Don't take advantage of a poor lonely woman."

Then she was on me shouting: "Oh, you're a wicked man, a wicked, wicked man. Oh, Wilfred . . . "

Beneath the bed an entire orchestra seemed to be tuning up. The frost patterns on the windows melted. Vaguely I wondered if the neighbours were observing us through binoculars; perhaps one of them would be called as a witness when I was charged with rape.

The situation was saved by Pepi who suddenly burst through the half-open door and tried to bite me in the private parts. I extricated myself and fled to the bathroom where, with sudden perception, I realised what had brought on Wilfred's heart attack.

When I went down for breakfast I found a note beside the grapefruit. PLEASE ACCEPT A WEEK'S NOTICE. I ONLY ACCOMMODATE GENTLEMEN.

Within half an hour I was on my way out of the house, worldly goods packed once more in the cardboard suitcase. As I walked down the garden path I heard her confiding to Pepi: "Gentlemen don't wear socks in bed."

* * *

During this traumatic domestic period I was also coping with the transition from weekly to daily journalism.

The *Eastern Daily Press* is a fine newspaper and I was extremely fortunate to have landed a job there. Its international and local coverage were comprehensive, its photographs were of a remarkably high standard, but its great strength was its leader-page articles and essays. I submitted about a dozen of these but none was ever published.

The King's Lynn office was in the High Street, a modern premises with stuttering neon lights; circulation and advertising in the front, editorial in the rear.

Four of us worked in this single room typing thunderously, putting in calls to village outposts, phoning copy to Norwich, slurping tea.

In one corner sat Terry Hutson, West Norfolk News Editor, rugged-faced and immaculately-suited; in the far corner sat Frank Keeler, the epitome of the best type of provincial journalist, prodigiously fast — I once saw smoke rising from his typewriter but it turned out to be a cigarette end — accurate and hard-working; squeezed in between the two were myself and Francis Rose who specialised in sport, but turned his hand to general news which he recorded in sprinting shorthand that at times seemed in danger of overtaking his pencil.

The three of them were exceedingly kind and it was from them that I finally learned what the newspaper business was all about.

At first, having observed my shorthand, my two-fingered typing, my cuttings from the column *Here There and Everywhere Round Dartmouth,* they employed me cautiously: the shipping lists from King's Lynn docks, prices from the Corn Exchange, table tennis notes every Wednesday, vegetable shows, amateur dramatics . . .

There came a time when I could have sung *The Gondoliers* and *The Mikado* backwards. I couldn't really pan these shows. In the first place my theatrical background was limited to a war-time visit to the Whitehall Theatre to see Phyllis Dixey in the nude; and in the second place the productions were so well-intentioned, the cast so obviously enjoying themselves, that it would have been cruel to criticise. The most damning plaudit was "A convincing performance was given by — " implying that the actor had muffed most of his lines and the remainder had been inaudible.

The most memorable performance was the opening night of *Rose Marie.* I sat in the stalls writing it up, making a show with my notebook so that the rest of the audience would realise that there was a critic among them. Down from London, perhaps, looking for talent!

The performance jogged along predictably — if you ignored the fact that one of the mounties was wearing a trilby because the costumiers had short-changed them by one hat — until the Indian Love Call. The baritone was in splendid form but, as he reached for the higher notes, the quality of his voice suddenly changed dramatically. A few notes later and it was back to normal; he seemed unaffected and the rest of the cast carried on as though nothing untoward had occurred.

I determined to solve the mystery. Perhaps there was a story here, perhaps something to titillate the national newspapers, Fleet Street aspirations having completely recovered from the chickenpox. It seemed as if another personality suddenly took over the body of the amply-proportioned baritone; perhaps Caruso had once sung here; although, considering the draughty, Dettol-smelling hall with its rows of classroom chairs, this seemed unlikely.

I waited anxiously for the baritone's next number. But his voice remained stable for the rest of the performance. It was only during the Indian Love Call that the phenomenon occurred.

My review was published in the EDP next morning. The baritone was "in fine voice." So was Rose Marie — "The usual competent performance we have come to expect." And one "convincing performance" for one of the stars who, overcome by first-night nerves, had suddenly lapsed into a number from *The Desert Song*.

The following evening I went to the stage door, gave the doorman a shilling, and wandered backstage where the mounties were getting stuck into a crate of light ale. No one took much notice of me.

The Indian Love Call was due to begin and I made my way as discreetly as possible to the wings where I found a fat man sitting on a packing case reading the *Beano*.

I whispered good evening to him and he looked up and said: "Evening, matey."

From behind us somewhere came a savage "Shush."

He shrugged his shoulders.

On stage the baritone was about to launch into the Love Call. A poignant moment, a beautiful song. But I wanted my story. I whispered to the fat man: "Can you spare a moment?"

He put his finger to his lips.

"Can I see you later?"

His answer was unexpected.

He stood up and unleashed three deafening notes of song.

On stage the baritone opened and shut his mouth noiselessly. Then, as the fat man finished, he took up the melody again.

It transpired that the baritone was quite unable to hit those particular notes and the fat man had been conscripted from a building site to help out.

I contemplated writing a story. But no, they were all far too nice.

* * *

After a while I was entrusted with more responsible jobs. The juvenile court, the occasional tribunal, annual general meetings and dinners with unvariable menus — consommé or fruit juice/roast chicken, creamed potatoes and peas/peach melba or cheese/coffee.

But the most pleasurable assignments were with our photographer, Claud Fisher. Claud was, I suppose, in his early sixties, a chubby-faced, balding perfectionist whose portraits of East Anglian life should be collected and exhibited.

With his big plate camera he isolated the ingredients of desolate rural beauty: an arrowhead of wild-fowl over marshland; a village cosseted in snow; the spire of a church reaching for a cloud; guildhalls and windmills and lonely mansions. If you looked at one of Claud's pictures of the River Ouse you could hear the water sucking at the mud.

Claud, a bachelor and authority on the Roman Catholic

Church, was not above doing the routine stint. Presentations, prize-givings, weddings, church parades. But even then his lens seemed to find moments of dignity unnoticed by his competitors.

Claud could also be extremely irascible and, if he disagreed with some edict from head office, it was advisable to steal quietly away from the office to the coffee shop across the street.

Occasionally I accompanied him to Sandringham when George VI and Queen Elizabeth and the two princesses were in residence. Sandringham was an oasis of parkland; lawns jewelled with frost, deep woods and holly with blood-red berries. It was also a feudal anachronism where gamekeepers still doffed their caps and peasants touched their forelocks.

It was at its baronial best at Christmas. I had visions of giant turkeys turning on the spit, Havana cigar smoke in the air, a Christmas tree as straight as a spear dressed in folds of tinsel, dogs everywhere, the spirits of Queen Victoria and Mr. Pickwick collaborating.

And outside the first timid flakes of snow.

I only saw Royalty when they attended Church on Christmas morning and Claud took their photographs while they smiled at him as though he were family. The King and Queen seemed to me to be as friendly and dignified as any couple could hope to be. The smile of the Queen, now the Queen Mother, still brightens the most turgid occasion; the King died in his sleep at Sandringham. But their regal togetherness in those leisurely days in East Anglia has been captured forever through Claud Fisher's lens.

IX

Speed. That was the overriding difference between the old order and the new. Whereas at Dartmouth there had been plenty of time in which to decipher notes, compose an intro and check the facts, I now had to deliver the goods with bewildering speed.

Telephoning copy to the *Evening News* was the real test of stamina and reflex. You emerged from the magistrates' court with a sheaf of notes about some complex motoring case; you had to cut the evidence by half without giving unfair prominence to defence or prosecution; you had to compose the punchiest intro possible; you had only five minutes flat in which to pass it on to Norwich because the King's Lynn edition went first.

But the compensations were intoxicating. To see the copies of the paper, still wet from the presses, dumped on the counter of the front office within five hours of your dictation; to see your story beneath a fat headline on the front page; to saunter along the High Street and observe homeward-bound citizens glancing at your prose . . . This is an exclusive ecstacy that only newspapermen can experience. To see your first book in print is another heady moment but I am not sure that even that compares with that first LOCAL MOTORIST BANNED FOR TWO YEARS FOR 'OUTRAGEOUS DRIVING' on the front page of an evening paper.

Not all the stories deserved front-page prominence: it was

merely that the front and back pages were last off the presses and so they were the only slots available for late news phoned from King's Lynn. The copy then had to be subbed and set in type before the presses rolled; then the papers had to be transported many miles to King's Lynn.

Readers often complain about typographical errors in newspapers, particularly in first editions, the most common being a transposition of a slug of type. *The Chairman congratulated Smith on his fine example* followed by *"He hit me with a bottle of HP sauce," said his wife* — that sort of thing. In fact, taking into consideration the speed of the operation, it is the relative rarity of mistakes that should confound.

In the speed stakes no one could compete with Francis Rose, a neat man with thinning hair and a gaberdine raincoat, who would pick up the telephone, chatter away to some official of King's Lynn Football Club (The Linnets), scrawl a few hieroglyphics on the nearest available scrap of paper, replace the receiver, pick it up again, dial Norwich and dictate an immaculate sports story.

But not even his speed could cope with the early rounds of the FA Cup when the national Sunday newspapers requested coverage. Thus on one fateful occasion he recklessly sought my help.

These early rounds of the Cup can be the most exhilarating of all. When a small non-league team takes on one of the League giants and either manages to salvage a draw or, miraculously, to beat them.

This year the Linnets had drawn a League team. So up to King's Lynn — or Lynn as it was tersely and affectionately known — came the national sports writers to write preliminary features.

I observed them with awe as they consulted Francis Rose. A raffish, likeable lot whose tobacco coughs and beer belches had no obvious connection with Olympian endeavour.

They all penned extremely readable stories because a little 'un taking on a big 'un always has hypnotic attraction. Then they departed to report on other matches since, despite their guarded predictions that David *might* trounce Goliath, none of them had much doubt that the Linnets would be obliterated.

On the Saturday morning Francis Rose took me to the coffee shop and regarded me dubiously. Sport was his domain and he didn't take kindly to intruders; but this time there was no alternative: not even he, with his winged pencil, could cope with so many commitments.

"Did you ever play football?"

"Rugby," I said, bowing my head.

He appeared to be in pain: rugby was only just a sport. "Not soccer?"

I shook my head. I loved sport but I was born a spectator.

"But you know a bit about it?"

"A bit," I said.

"Enough to write two hundred and fifty words and phone it to one of the Sundays?"

I made the sort of open-handed gesture that can have several interpretations.

He sipped his coffee, then snapped: "Explain the off-side rule."

I mumbled something about no-one being between the player with the ball and the goal.

Francis moaned softly. Then he brightened. "Could you just phone the result to Ex Tel?"

"You mean you don't want me to write anything?"

"That's right," said Francis who was forthright to a fault.

I tried to hide my disappointment. I had always wanted to write a sports report and get a little poetry into it, not conced-

98

ing that the last thing your average sports reader wants is purple passages mixed up with the goal scorers.

"It's bloody important," Francis said.

Which it was. In those days Exchange Telegraph, one of the big news agencies, transmitted the football results to the BBC and to all the leading newspapers. The football punter with seven draws already recorded, hysterically waiting for the eighth result, was dependent upon Exchange Telegraph which was dependent upon its correspondent covering the match. Mercurial speed was of the essence on a Saturday afternoon as, all over the country, the presses thumped out sporting editions in standard white newsprint or, in the provinces, in pink, green and, I believe, yellow in a few outposts.

"You'll have to use an outside telephone," Francis told me. "All the Press phones will be in use. Get yourself an accomplice."

"An accomplice?"

Francis shook his head in exasperation; I half expected him to ask me if they had taught me about accomplices in my correspondence course.

He said: "To occupy a telephone kiosk. You can't phone the result if some bugger's talking to his bird, can you?" He finished his coffee. "And there aren't all that many phone boxes in the Walks," the parkland where the football ground was situated. "So get yourself an accomplice. Stick him in a kiosk ten minutes before you're due to phone and make him stay there. Give him a couple of bob," Francis added, airily disposing of my Saturday night beer money.

Exchange Telegraph might have argued that, in view of their commitment to the waiting millions, they should have had priority over the Press telephones, but that wasn't the way local newspapermen saw it: top priority was their Pink 'un or Green 'un, and the big agencies and London newspapers would have to take their turn.

And, of course, feeding the local sporting editions was nerve-wracking business. First a few paragraphs setting the scene followed by team changes, then half-a-dozen paragraphs phoned at set intervals, then the half-time scores, finally the full-time score and a few wrap-up paragraphs. All this had to be performed while the crowd bayed, while incidents occurred at the far end of a fog-shrouded pitch, while lightning goals were scored by visiting players whom you could only identify by the numbers on their backs.

Wrist watches were a great help in maintaining a flowing report, hence the frequency of "In the eighteenth minute Spicer slipped a low pass to Wilkinson who hit the woodwork" or "In the fortieth minute Wilkinson scored an own goal after a misunderstanding with Spicer." Those who criticise a certain predictability of style in these reports should pause and consider the conditions under which they are written.

And then they should consider the conditions in which they are produced — a battery of part-time copy-takers with headphones typing correspondent's reports, the copy snatched from the typewriter by a copy-boy and rushed to a sports sub-editor who knocks it into shape and writes the headlines and subheads, subbed copy spirited to the Linotype operators and then to the stone and then to the presses and then into the waiting vans with Grand Prix drivers at the wheels to be transported to far-flung outposts. King's Lynn was so far-flung from Norwich that the sports edition had to be dispatched before the end of the game; the result — and all the other results — had to be typed onto a stencil at King's Lynn and printed in the fudge (the stop-press) on a copying machine under the supervision of the West Norfolk circulation manager, Alf Goff, a grey-haired *young* man of tremendous vitality.

It was small wonder, then, that mistakes occurred; that portions of one match sometimes appeared in the middle of another, occasionally in the middle of a different sporting event. Thus: King's Lynn 2, Australia 385 for 4.

But the intricacies of production were far from my mind that raw winter day with an iced wind keening in from the fens, roofs shining like fish scales after the night's rain, starlings pecking in muddy gardens.

I had to find an accomplice. Who would be willing to stand in a telephone kiosk for twenty minutes — ten before half-time, ten before full-time — on a cold dank day for a remuneration of two shillings? On any other day it might have been possible to find a volunteer: not on the day that the Linnets had drawn a Third Division league side at home.

Finally I settled on a well-nourished boy who lived next door to my digs. He had little interest in football, only eating. I gave him two shillings and a Mars bar.

I reported early to the football ground to get the feel of it. The paths across the Walks swarmed with supporters wearing mufflers and woollen hats in King's Lynn colours. These were the stalwarts who attended every match to glory or despair in the Linnets' achievements, to identify with those eleven granite-thighed athletes, to exult, cherry-nosed and cloth-capped, at an afternoon's freedom from assembly line or office. Among them this afternoon were the fringe fans who came twice a year — and had treacherously forecast this match as an away win.

I know of no preliminary — except, perhaps, an orchestral overture in some gilded, high-ceilinged theatre — as exciting as the build-up to a big soccer match. There is tension abroad, cameraderie and escape; and the emotion is as raw as neat spirit, especially when the weather is bleak with the smell of snow or fog in the air because this, as every fan knows, is true football weather. Who wants Mediterranean skies and the scent of blossom on the breeze? No, let us feel the snapping gums of winter; this is a test of endurance for player and fan, the pleasure touched with masochism.

But after the ecstatic ordeal — if the home team has won — there are cosy delights ahead: the match replayed over a couple of pints, coal-fire glowing at home and ham salad for supper, and bell-chiming, roast-in-the-oven Sunday waiting in the wings.

I showed my Press ticket at the gate and went in self-consciously. Most of the opposition fans had already arrived and were grouped together as lordly and patronising as dandies at a dog fight. They pointed out the modest facilities of the ground, and laughed hugely. Was their journey really necessary?

I inspected the Press box. Sports writers from newspapers in the visitors' home town were already installed, phoning their offices, studying the programme.

A scratched record of Donald Peers singing *Powder Your Face With Sunshine* was being relayed through the loudspeakers.

Francis Rose arrived beaming — this was his day — although the beam slipped a little when he saw me. "Have you got your — ?"

"My accomplice is stationed outside," I said.

He nodded thoughtfully.

Team changes were announced over the loudspeakers; the sports writers amended their programmes.

The terraces were packed.

Then the two teams pranced onto the pitch, posed obligingly for kneeling photographers and began to kick footballs around with graces unimpeded by bone-crunching tackles.

The whistle blew. The game was on. The crowd roared, sighed and groaned. And there was no trouble. My memory may have become sugared over the years but I do know that, in those days, you could send your son to a football match with-

102

out the slightest fear that he would be beaten up — or killed — by some pathetic moron wearing bovver boots.

I went outside to check on my accomplice. He had finished his Mars bar and was demanding another. I slipped him a threepenny piece and told him that, if he played his part, I would buy him a bag of fish and chips later.

From outside the ground I heard the roars of the crowd rising and falling, an exhilarating but usually inaccurate barometer of play.

I returned to the gate just before half-time. The arrangement was that Frank Keeler, who was helping Francis Rose phone reports rather than mere results, would slip me the scores which I would rush to the telephone kiosk.

And it all went with oiled precision. The boy vacated the kiosk and I put in a transfer-charge call to Exchange Telegraph.

"Who's that, old boy?"

"Rose of King's Lynn."

"Okay, old boy, shoot."

The first indication that the oil was running dry in the operation came when I returned to the pitch and the man at the gate asked for my pass and I discovered that I had lost it. However, he remembered my face and let me in after a few morose comments about the local Press.

I couldn't see anything but I could hear the sound of boot against ball, the sighs and shouts of the crowd. And I could see my fellow Pressmen scribbling, talking earnestly into their telephones.

Here I was, an integral part of the operation. The whole country — the world — waited for my call: within seconds my information would be relayed from the telephone box in the Walks to London, Johannesburg, Melbourne . . .

I trembled at the responsibility.

Then a great roar, cheering, clapping. What in God's name had happened? Desperately I searched for Frank Keeler. And there he was gesturing from the Press box. I advanced nearer.

"Extra time."

"What?"

"Extra bloody time."

I headed for the telephone kiosk. This was something I hadn't bargained for. Nor had my accomplice. "You told me — "

"I know I did," I said, pulling him out of the kiosk.

"Who's that, old boy?" asked the copy-taker.

"Rose of King's Lynn."

"Okay, old boy, shoot."

"Extra time — "

"What's that, old man?"

"Extra — "

"No, old man, the score — "

Finally he got the message and I left the kiosk to confront my accomplice.

He said: "So that's it. What about the fish and chips?"

"No," I replied carefully, "that's not quite it."

His stomach rumbled. "What do you mean that's not quite it?"

"They're playing extra time."

"You never said anything — "

"I didn't know — " And then before he could protest any further: "Two pieces of cod and two portions of chips if you see this thing through."

"All right," he said, "but my mother — "

"I'll explain it to your mother," I said.

So now Britain, the world, punters with hundreds of thousands of pounds at stake were dependent upon the promise of an extra piece of cod and a bonus of chips.

I headed back to the pitch. Roars, shrieks and groans as the little 'uns gave as good as they got and the superior smiles slid from their supporters' faces.

Then it was all over.

Icy-cheeked faces poured out of the ground as, swimming against the tide I tried to reach Frank Keeler. What was the result? God in heaven I didn't even know.

"What was the score?" I asked as the tide of faces swept past me in the dusk, but no one bothered with a fool trying to stand against a triumphant exodus. Or was it triumphant?

Then I saw Frank Keeler, his handsome, Alan Ladd face never more welcome.

"Two all," he shouted, or something like that.

"What?"

"Two all." Being the efficient fellow he was he thrust a scrap of paper in my hand: Two all.

I sprinted towards the telephone kiosk, my office.

But I wasn't office manager, not of that particular kiosk. Inside it was a large, crew-cut American airman talking to his girl-friend.

My accomplice said: "He threw me out."

"We'll see about that," I said. Anglo-American relations had never been too happy in King's Lynn. I pulled open the door and said: "Excuse me, I think this kiosk was occupied."

He clapped one enormous hand over the receiver. "What do you want, kid?"

"This gentleman" — pointing at my accomplice — "was in possession of the kiosk."

"Was he now?"

"And if you'd kindly vacate — "

"Vacate? What's all this shit?"

"Vacate," I said. "Leave. Quit."

"Quit shit," he remarked.

"I've got to get a soccer result over . . . "

"Sucker?"

"No, soccer."

"Man, I don't know what the hell you're talking about," closing the heavy door of the kiosk.

I managed to pull open the door again. All over Britain the final results had been received. All that the panters were waiting for were the results of the extra-times. By now most of these must have been telephoned.

One score not recorded. The BBC waiting for the blank in their classified results. Football-pool competitors waiting for the score that could realise them fortunes . . .

The American was saying: "But Jesus, baby — "

"Excuse me," I said.

Once again he put his hand over the receiver. "Why don't you — off, kid."

Fury began to cloud my vision. Adrenalin flowed. But the last spectators were leaving the ground.

The world waited . . . I envisaged a household utterly dependent on this last result.

Oh, Christ!

On the far side of the Walks I spotted an empty kiosk. Shouting to the American: "You wait, I'll be back," I sprinted across the muddy turf and hurled myself into the kiosk.

I dialled the operator and waited. Nothing. There hadn't even been a dialling tone! Then I noticed that the wire had been wrenched from its fitting.

Now sheer panic set in. I raced across the expanses of the Walks mumbling to myself. Disgrace. Humiliation. Failure.

And still the world waited while I, a wild-eyed maniac, ran across a park in West Norfolk without the slightest idea whether a telephone box lay ahead.

I imagined the scene at Exchange Telegraph as they waited

for the one missing result. I imagined the BBC announcer reaching the King's Lynn game and stumbling over the blank space. I imagined a domestic scene where a widower, father of seven needy children, himself dying of tuberculosis, waited for the one result that could bring salvation. "Daddy, daddy, have we won?"

"I don't know, little one." Hands trembling, sweat beading his brow.

"Papa, papa, will we have a beautiful house in the country?"

Papa doesn't answer: Papa is unconscious on the floor.

I ran on, arms working like pistons, pain knifing my chest. Then in front of me, a red oasis in a desert of mud and grass, a kiosk. I knew at that moment how a shipwrecked survivor feels when he sees a rescue plane circling overhead.

I fell panting into the kiosk, dialled the operator and put through my transfer charge call to London.

"Give me copy."

But I was put straight through to the sports desk. "Where have you been, old man?"

I panted into the phone.

"Steady on, old man, are you all right?"

Yes, I said, I was all right.

"Okay, old man, let's have it."

The score! What was the bloody score? I searched my pockets; dimly I remembered handing my accomplice Frank Keeler's scrap of paper while I wrenched open the door of the kiosk where the American was in residence.

"The score, old man. You're last. We've been waiting — "

What the hell had Frank Keeler said? I tried to memorise his lip movements. Dear God, help me and I shall go to church every Sunday until I'm ninety.

I took a deep breath and said: "Two all."

Intake of breath. "Another draw."

107

"Yes," I said, "another draw."

I put down the phone and began the long walk back across the Walks. Had it been two all? If not, then I would drink a bottle of whisky — except that I couldn't afford it — and jump into the Ouse.

I pictured my tubercular widower rising from the floor and embracing his children. "Little ones, we're saved." And then discovering later that the result had been a home win . . .

I stopped a boy wearing a Linnets' scarf. "Who won?" I asked grinning horribly.

"No one," he said.

"A draw?"

He nodded. "Two all."

I almost embraced him.

On the way home I heard a radio through the half-open door of a house. "And now a late result . . . "

X

Throughout this period I was writing regular letters of application to the editors and news editors of national newspapers. Fleet Street was Mecca: somehow or other I had to get there.

My ambition was whetted by the arrival of Pressmen from all over the world to cover the death of the King. I had in a way prepared them for his death because, during his convalescence from a lung operation, I had telephoned a daily paragraph about his shooting expeditions to the agencies in London.

One day he didn't go shooting: the next day he was dead.

On the day of his death I received a phone call from the *Star,* a London evening paper now defunct. "Can you describe the scene," said a pleading voice.

"I haven't been up there." In fact I was looking after routine business while Frank Keeler, Francis Rose, Terry Hutson and Claud Fisher covered the scene at Sandringham.

"No, the scene in King's Lynn. The King was pretty well-known there — "

"He was pretty well-known everywhere," I said.

"The Royal family used to go shopping in King's Lynn. After all it is *King's* Lynn." He paused. "Take a look out of the window and tell me what you can see."

I walked into the advertising and circulation office and stared out through the window. Flags were flying at half mast, women were dressed in black, men wore black armbands, an old lady reading the *Eastern Daily Press* was crying, some shops had closed, there were black-bordered notices in the windows.

I told the man from the *Star* what I had seen and it made half a column. And so I learned how to improvise with scanty material.

Later that day I accompanied Frank Keeler to Sandringham in the office car. And there was the world's Press — sitting in the back of chauffeur-driven limousines punching out stories on portable typewriters, lodged in telephone boxes, overflowing from hotels and pubs. Reporters, photographers with their big Speed Graphic plate cameras, wire-room operators waiting to transmit pictures to London.

There, too, were the feature *writers*. Journalists with a descriptive flare which hard-news reporters are not expected to possess — unless they are the newspaper's lone representative in some remote corner of the world when a feature editor may suddenly reassess their capabilities.

The reporting of events during those few sad days at Sandringham was of a high quality. But the most traumatic story was a report by a reporter who had recently left one national newspaper to join a rival. Now Fleet Street phone numbers are mostly simple, easy to memorise, and they lodge in a reporter's brain for his life-span.

The reporter in question telephoned a long and eloquent piece to a copy-taker before asking to be transferred to the news desk to receive the plaudits that he believed were his due.

"A great piece," said a familiar voice on the other end of the phone.

The reporter smiled happily into the receiver.

"There's only one thing . . . "

"You want some more?"

"*We* don't," said the voice. "But your new paper might. You left us last week. Remember?"

* * *

While the national newspapermen were in the area I obtained from them the names of their editors and news editors and dispatched a further batch of application letters. If the editors regarded the regularity of my applications as tiresome then, I admonished them gently, they should remember that tenacity was part of a good reporter's equipment.

One news editor responded with a little more than the routine rejection and invited me to London for an interview. His name was Ken Hord, he was news editor of the *Daily Mirror* and he was one of the most formidable and competent newspaper executives in Fleet Street.

Cool, pale-haired, grey-suited, he looked more like a schoolmaster than the news editor of a brash tabloid, featuring a strip cartoon like *Jane,* rarely fully-clothed, and news items of sometimes astonishing content.

For instance the lavatory attendant who kept goldfish in the glass cisterns. And the classic account of the unfortunate man who left a bottle of Gloy beside his bath. Having bathed himself satisfactorily he stood up, slipped and fell on top of the conical bottle which immediately disappeared. Being a resourceful man he dressed, mounted his motor-cycle and drove to the nearest hospital where the Gloy bottle was removed. The report appeared under the headline AN UNFORTUNATE ACCIDENT.

The *Mirror* also carried fine, fighting leaders and was the champion of victimised servicemen. It was largely the serviceman's vote that brought in the Labour Government after the war and it was, to a large extent, the *Mirror* that influenced the servicemen.

The *Mirror's* legendary editor was Sylvester Bolam, jailed for six months for an injudicious headline concerning proceedings against acid-bath murderer Haig. When I reported to the

111

Mirror offices Jack Nener, silver-haired, bow-tied, the archetypal editor with a voice like a buzz-saw, had taken over and Hugh Cudlipp, the Welsh wizard — one of three brothers, all Fleet Street editors — was in overall charge. But such men were as remote from me as the stars.

I sat in the small room outside the editorial floor waiting to be interviewed by Ken Hord, as austere as Jack Nener and Hugh Cudlipp were flamboyant. The sliding door opened and Ken Hord entered, sat down, crossed his legs and surveyed me. All pretensions withered; that was the effect he had on people; a lie hung between you like a deflating balloon until he finished it off with a single thrusting question. He was friendly enough; but so is a cross-examining QC luring you into an indiscretion.

He had asked for cuttings and I handed them to him hopelessly. HERE THERE AND EVERYWHERE IN BRIXHAM. Hardly seemed likely to depose Cassandra; nor, for that matter, did RED MOUNT'S LINES FROM LYNN, a column which I occasionally wrote when Frank Keeler was away.

He thumbed through them reflectively. Then said: "Show me the one cutting that you're most proud of."

A difficult proposition because I was ashamed of the whole shabang. I had spent hours agonising over my choice until, in desperation, I had considered including some of Frank Keeler's or Francis Rose's better pieces. Thank God I hadn't, not in this inquisitorial presence.

I said: "I haven't really had a chance to write anything in the *Mirror* style."

He nodded impatiently. "Just one cutting, Mr. Lambert."

I handed him RED MOUNT'S LINES which were far from immortal. A treatise, in fact, on the nourishing qualities of fish and chips, the importance of fish in news-gathering having been indelibly imprinted on my brain since that first interview for the *Dartmouth Chronicle*.

He began to read, painstakingly rather than avidly. He was saved by the appearance of a grey-haired lady whom I was subsequently to know as Dot Watson, Ken Hord's grey eminence. She told him that he was wanted urgently.

I waited miserably in the hire-and-fire room wishing I had made some spectacular application for a job like the one perpetrated by Tommy Clayton.

He had sent a telegram to Arthur Christiensen, fabled editor of the *Daily Express*, saying "I AM THE MAN YOU WANT" and adding that he would be in a Fleet Street pub at such and such a time.

A message duly reached the pub and later that day Tommy Clayton faced the great man who said: "So you're the man I want?"

"Yes, sir," said Tommy.

Christiensen reached for the telephone, talked to his foreign editor, then turned to Clayton and said: "You fly to Cairo at six this evening."

Which he did — and served the *Express* honourably for many years.

Ken Hord returned and told me that there had been a spectacular murder in Essex. I imagined reporters and photographers speeding on their way, saw the big black headlines next day ... And here I was with RED MOUNT'S LINES FROM LYNN.

He glanced once more at the cutting, handed it back to me and said: "Tell me about yourself."

What was there to tell? I was the man responsible for the smallpox scare that turned out to be chickenpox; I was the man who had caused football pool enthusiasts all over the country to have apoplexy.

"Come on, chum" — chum was his favourite address although it wasn't necessarily chummy — "Tell me what makes you tick."

I embarked on my insipid life story, barging around its confines like a trapped bluebottle until he interrupted: "Are you fond of sport?" A gleam in his eye.

"Yes," I said. Pray God he doesn't ask me about the off-side rule.

"Cricket?"

"Cricket is my favourite game."

The gleam sharpened. "We have a team here. We play the *Express* once a year."

"I've played a bit," I said, hoping he would interpret this totally truthful statement as British understatement.

"Batting or bowling? Or" — hopefully — "both?"

"I bowl a bit," I said. *Mostly in the back garden.*

"Mmmmmm." He became once more the professional interrogator. "What sort of bowling?"

"Off-breaks," I said wildly.

"I see." And, with terrible precision: "How do you hold the ball?"

I waggled my hand in front of him, twisting my fingers.

"Perfect," he said.

I sat back smugly: I had managed to deceive this cool professional whose ancestry stretched back to the Spanish inquisitors — in fact, as I was later to discover, one of the most fair-minded and kindly men in Fleet Street.

"Perfect," he repeated. "If you wanted to bowl a *leg*-break." He stood up. "Thank you for coming to see us, Mr. Lambert." He stuck out his hand. "Try us again when you've had a little more experience," and was gone.

In the forecourt of the old pagoda-like building in Fetter Lane, a few hundred yards from Fleet Street, reinforcements for the Essex murder were piling into a black Humber Hawk.

I screwed up RED MOUNT'S LINES FROM LYNN into a tight ball and threw them into the gutter.

XI

My first brush with death occurred beside a flooded ditch on the outskirts of a Norfolk village.

Two boys sailing paper boats found the body of a fourteen-year-old girl lying in the water, her long hair floating like seaweed. I was in the area covering a rural district council meeting and was present when the body was fished from the ditch.

She had been raped and strangled and her face still bore an expression of ultimate fear and incomprehension as her life was taken from her. One minute feeling the breeze from the fens on her face, perhaps on her way to meet her first boyfriend, the next minute maniacally savaged, and then dead. It wasn't so much the fact of death that chilled me, but that look of incomprehension — the trust of the young betrayed.

The village constable laid the body, scarcely buddied, on the grass verge among the dandelions — her first wreaths — and covered it with a blanket. I telephoned the story to Norwich, the face of the girl floating in my vision.

Within hours a superintendent and a sergeant from Scotland Yard had arrived in the village, followed by a retinue of crime reporters barely distinguishable from the detectives.

The reporters were an impressive bunch and, from the wings, I watched them at work. Each contrived to have a secret meet, as they called it, with the superintendent or his assistant. Each assiduously cultivated the village constable and, on occasions, myself, in the optimistic belief, soon dispelled, that I might know a thing or two. Each was a curious mixture of conviviality and secrecy, buying expensive rounds in the pub before disappearing on clandestine missions; when they returned they exuded optimism and were plied with drinks by nervous competitors sensing that they had missed an exclusive. They hunted in a pack and yet at the same time they were loners.

When the superintendent, whom they all addressed by his Christian name, was in expansive mood they clustered round him forming an impenetrable wall which excluded even general-news reporters from their own newspapers. If a general reporter did manage to infiltrate and ask an embarrassing question such as: "Do you know the identity of the murderer?" they shuffled uneasily and apologised on his behalf. Questions were always oblique, the replies couched in a mysterious patois in which no one was ever named and nothing definitive was ever stated. If, for example "the chief monkey had been sussed for GBH" I assumed, after considerable deliberation, that the principal suspect had been previously under suspicion for grevious bodily harm.

This was the era when murders were always big news, only edged off the front page by elopements to Gretna Green. The Scotland Yard detectives, squarely-built, authoritative and intimidating, were household names and so were the crime reporters.

Among the best — possibly a little subsequent to this period — was Rodney Hallworth of the *Daily Mail*, a generously-proportioned *prima donna,* intimate with such legendary detectives as Charlie Capstick and Bert Hannam, who frequently pinched exclusives from under the tankards of his competitors and liked to dictate his stories from a hotel bedroom, prowling around with yards of telephone wire unravelling behind him,

116

flourishing a Manniken cigar and delivering his story with the ringing authority of a North Country Lawrence Olivier.

Other leaders among this troupe who travelled the land from crime to crime in the fifties and sixties — some still on the trail — were Owen Summers of the *Daily Sketch*, now with the *Express,* a man of cherubic charm and finely-honed news instincts; Tom Sandrock, still with the *Daily Telegraph,* as dependable as the tides; Peter Stewart of the *Sketch,* latterly BBC, a reporter of great presence who ruthlessly pursued a story until it surrendered; Bob Traini of the *Daily Herald* and Reg "Fireman" Foster of the *News Chronicle,* inseparable friends despite the demands of rival newspapers; Tom Tullet of the *Daily Mirror,* who looked more like a detective superintendent than the detective superintendents; Howard Johnson, chief reporter of the *Mirror,* the most courteous reporter in the game; Dickie Herd of the London *Evening News,* the most immaculate of the bunch; Alf Draper of the *Herald,* the least immaculate but certainly one of the best.

The doyen was Percy Hoskins of the *Daily Express* who looked like Alfred Hitchcock, operated from a flat in Park Lane and got his tips from the hierarchy of Scotland Yard. But the best, in my opinion, was Donald Seaman, also of the *Express,* who covered wars as well as crimes — a prickly, tenacious character with a brilliant turn of phrase. If Seaman, utterly dedicated to the *Express,* arrived on a story the opposition dispatched two reporters to bring them up to par; these days he is a successful novelist living in voluntary exile in Cornwall.

They were an awesome bunch to me, the man from the *EDP*, specialist in dog shows, amateur dramatics and corn prices; I was fascinated by their techniques, astonished at their consumption of Scotch. I would readily have polished their shoes and run their copy for them; but in their eyes I barely existed.

117

The story of the murdered girl ran its allotted course, a journalistic formula which I had yet to appreciate. The discovery of the body, interviews with a prime suspect claiming "I've got nothing to hide", detectives mingling with mourners at the funeral, appeals to the public to come forward, reconstruction of the murder a week later. No one was arrested and the story was demoted to the inside pages finally shrinking to a few paragraphs among the truss-ads at the foot of the pages.

On the day the Scotland Yard team was preparing to return to base, I slipped into the village pub which had taken more money in two weeks than it normally did in two years and ordered myself a half pint of bitter, served to me with disdain by a barman who had become accustomed to pouring large whiskies.

I was moodily sipping the beer when the superintendent from Scotland Yard walked in and bought himself a pint. I doubted whether he had ever noticed me but I was wrong. Perhaps I had even been a suspect.

He nodded in my direction. "A beer?"

I accepted the drink, noting the change in the barman's demeanour, and tried to think of a question to ask, something subtle but pertinent and at the same time jovial. Nothing surfaced.

The detective, barrel-chested, city-suited, his face seamed by daily contact with human treachery, lit his pipe and said: "Your first big crime story?"

I had in fact only been assisting but I didn't go into detail. "My first murder," I said.

"A nasty one, too. I've got a daughter of that age." He sank half his pint with three gulps. "How old are you, son?"

"Twenty-two."

"Do you want to become a crime reporter?"

"I don't want to specialise," I told him. "I want to be able to

118

cover everything."

"Very sensible too. The spectrum of life. But you need the breaks just like everyone else." He pointed his pipe at me like a pistol. "And you've got to learn to stand up for yourself. Don't let this bunch intimidate you," pointing out of the window where a group of reporters were conferring in the winter sunlight. "You know something, I don't ever remember you asking a question."

I had, but no one had taken any notice of it.

"Well, the story's dead now." He smiled. "When the reporters pack it in I know it's time to go."

With one hand I was trying to count the change in my trouser pocket to see if I had enough money to buy him a drink.

But he sussed me. "Have another one on the Yard. And make it a pint," he said to the hovering barman. "I remember when I was on the beat," he said. "Come pay-day and I hadn't the price of a cup of coffee."

I was surprised at his kindliness, like finding soft loam beneath flints; similar to the astonishing discovery in your teens that schoolmasters and family doctors are fallible.

He emptied his tankard with another couple of swallows. "Well, we really turned this village over," he remarked.

"Do you think someone was shielding the murderer?" I asked.

"Come on," he said, "we had that story last week."

In fact I hadn't been asking professionally. There was a macabre fascination in the knowledge that one of the inhabitants of the hamlet, butcher, baker or candlestick-maker, was acting out the routines of life nursing his terrible guilt. What's more, life in the village tainted by suspicion would never be normal again until he was caught.

The phone in the corner of the bar rang. The barman picked it up and said: "It's for you, superintendent."

I made a performance of someone trying not to eavesdrop while the detective spoke in monosyllables. He returned thoughtfully to the bar.

Then he said to me: "You asked me a question just now."

"I asked if you thought someone was trying to shield the murderer," I said miserably.

The superintendent glanced at the barman who was also pantomiming someone trying not to listen. The superintendent beckoned me into the far corner of the bar.

"Well, someone was shielding him," he said. "But she isn't anymore. A kid of eighteen — his mother took him to the police station an hour ago."

"Here?" shivering with excitement.

"No, in Manchester. It seems that he nicked a car and drove down here. It might not stick, of course, but it looks as though you've got yourself a story, son."

Just then the crime reporters from Fleet Street entered in strength and, seeing the superintendent stuck with me in the corner, rushed to his aid.

One of them asked: "Anything fresh?"

The superintendent shook his head wearily. "Not a bloody thing," he said.

XII

By this time I had been joined in King's Lynn by a long-legged, green-eyed girl named Elizabeth whom I had met at the Four Hundred ballroom in Torquay. She was a girl of considerable fortitude because courtship with me was an unrewarding experience: I was always broke, the high spot of the week was a half of bitter in a pub and most evenings were interrupted by the demands of my profession.

During a romantic interlude — romance being a relative term in ice-sheathed lanes redolent of sugar-beet — I would remember the nightly telephone calls. I would break away from a passionate embrace and leg it to the nearest kiosk to ring up police, fire and ambulance.

These always involved badinage from the duty officers and took about ten minutes; but a ten-minute break can destroy a romantic interlude as effectively as an earth tremor. Occasionally there would be a story — a fire in a barn, an Anglo-American brawl in a public bar, a body in the Ouse — and I would dispatch Elizabeth back to her digs.

She was a girl of fiery temperament and didn't always understand that a collison between a car and a stray cow was of more importance than romance; but she was also a girl of sterling character and we survived.

She accompanied me to amateur theatricals — *Sister Bonaventure* seemed to predominate at that period — organ recitals, agricultural exhibitions, church services and pet shows.

On my days off we went for long walks in the flat, frozen countryside or took a bus to Heacham or Hunstanton, a sandy resort where, in those days, an alert freelance named Graham Fisher operated, landing many more stories in the national Press than the Lynn EDP staff because loyally we served our own newspapers first.

Although by this time I did have a few lineage sidelines to augment our joint income — Elizabeth had got a job as a secretary at a laundry. A few paragraphs in *Weekend Mail,* the sugarbeet prices in *Farmer's Weekly,* a couple of front page leads in *World's Fair,* the journal of market and fairground people, because the Mart, the first fair of the season, was held at Lynn. I also contributed to a magazine named *The Muck Spreader* but it seemed indelicate to confide to Elizabeth that it was *Muck Spreader* money that had paid for the half bottle of Algerian plonk with which we had washed down our sausages and chips.

I was paid three pounds and ten shillings a week and by payday we were both penniless. We possessed nothing except our clothes; no transport, not even a bicycle. Shoe repairs were a major item; threadbare clothes could only be replaced at saletime; on one triumphant occasion we bought Elizabeth a reversible coat, purple one side and black-and-white check the other, two coats for the price of one. I bought a blazer on the never-never from Hepworths to cover both formal and informal occasions, and a black overcoat of such lugubrious appearance that at funerals I was often mistaken for the undertaker.

Thus equipped we withstood the snows and mists of an East Anglian winter as it stretched long frozen fingers towards spring. And I continued to cover the routine processes of a small town which were as rhythmic and regular as the seasons. Magistrates' court twice a week, juvenile court, county court, council . . .

The magistrates' court provided the best insight into human weakness, although in Lynn these insights were often squalid. Young girls with cornflower blue eyes and delicate complexions, living in disorderly houses thick with filth committing "certain offences" in cat-squalling alleys ...

In the more serious cases, burglary or grevious bodily harm or arson, our chief of police, Superintendent Fred Calvert, prosecuted. He was a handsome, burly man with black hair as sleek as a cat's and he and his wife, Alice, were prominent in the amateur operatic society.

He was a good cop, was Fred Calvert, with a born instinct for publicity, which every police chief should have, although as No. 4 at the EDP, I rarely got a chance to speak to him.

But No. 4 was beginning to come into his own, trusted with some of the heavier engagements in the diary, writing the occasional LINES FROM LYNN which Frank Keeler, chain-smoking and machine-gunning his typewriter, produced twice a week with astonishing ease, wit and lyricism.

The only opposition to the EDP was the *Lynn News and Advertiser* which appeared twice a week giving us something approaching daily competition. My opposite number was a handsome, hawk-faced young man named Ray Perryman who sported green shirts and a Sherlock Holmes pipe.

We met several times a week and shared the more pedestrian duties, the most irksome of which was a committal for trial. Evidence was taken in depositions typed by a secretary, occasionally by the clerk to the court.

Defence lawyer: "I put it to you, sir, that the whole of your evidence has been a pack of lies, a web of fantasy, a fabrication."

Witness: "No."

And then, tap, tap, tap, question and answer.

Ray Perryman and I would either take notes for each other

while the one retired for a cup of tea or, if the evidence was undiluted tedium, we would rise together and leave the courtroom, a disconcerting spectacle for a lawyer in full flood.

After these laborious proceedings the deposition had to be read aloud. Then the lone magistrate delegated to listen to these tedious dualogues would, if he were still awake, confer with the clerk, announce that a *prima facie* case had been made out and commit the defendant for trial.

On one occasion, the magistrate did fall asleep. An alert young barrister leapt tigerishly to his feet and, quivering eagerly, shouted: "Objection."

The magistrate responded with a bubbling snore. When the clerk — the real power in any lay magistrates' court — prodded him he awoke abruptly, snapped "Objection overruled" and went back to sleep.

The trial took place at the quarter sessions a few weeks or months after the committal. And you had to listen to the whole rigmarole all over again, interrupted by cross-examination such as: "I put it to you, sir, that this isn't what you said in your original deposition."

The quarter sessions were awesome at first. The pageantry of the opening, the Recorder, God-like on the bench, bewigged barristers and bewildered jury.

One of the main objections to the jury system is the resentment of many of the jurors plucked from their workaday lives to serve the interests of justice for a pittance. Understandably their preoccupation is to get away as soon as possible.

On one occasion a simpleton stood in the dock accused of some routine crime of violence.

Half way through the prosecution the Recorder leaned forward to explain a point of law to the jury finishing with the words: "Do you understand?"

The foreman nodded, snapped to attention and, in the brisk

tones of a soldier reciting name and number before receiving his pay, announced: "Guilty, my lord."

* * *

Celebrities, with the exception of Royalty, were few and far between in King's Lynn, although I once interviewed Sir Osbert Sitwell when he spoke at Lynn Festival at the Guildhall.

He recalled his first public address when he arose, stricken with nerves, intending to say: "This is my first speech," and heard himself say: "This is my worst speech."

Sir Osbert apart, the only big name that I encountered was Noel Coward. It was my day off and I had dropped into the office to borrow ten shillings when the phone rang.

It was an anonymous tip-off. Noel Coward was staying in Downham Market, a small town eleven miles from King's Lynn. There was no one else in editorial so, quivering with initiative, I caught a bus to Downham.

Where would the great man be staying? Come to that what in heaven's name was he doing in Downham, hardly the locale for another *Blithe Spirit* or *Private Lives.* Perhaps a comedy of manners set in some ancestral home.

I might have a theatrical scoop on my hands. And a few barbed witticisms as a bonus.

The few inhabitants whom I questioned received the news that the darling of the British theatre was in town phlegmatically. No one knew where he was staying. I phoned a couple of ancestral homes; no luck — one woman told me that they never entertained theatricals.

I counted the coins in my pocket and headed for a pub where, in the public bar, I ordered a half of bitter reflecting that I should have been twirling a glass of Martini, very very dry.

In a stage whisper I asked the barman: "Have you any idea where Noel Coward is staying?"

Possibly the most improbable question ever put by a newspaperman in a public bar.

He looked up from the *Morning Advertiser*. "Who?"

I groaned. Then more loudly: "Noel Coward."

The barman nodded towards the corner of the bar.

I had vaguely been aware that there was another customer in the bar; now he emerged from the gloom, a small man with a sly face and a peaked cap several sizes too large for him.

"Are you the young gentleman from the local paper?" he asked.

I nodded. Perhaps Noel had sent an emissary — although he looked more like a race-course tipster.

"Took your time, didn't you?" he said.

"Did Mr. Coward sent you?"

The barman interrupted. "He *is* Mr. Coward."

"Aye, and I've got a birth certificate to prove it."

And he had.

XIII

Many tourists, misled by travel brochures, still believe that English villages are sleepy anachronisms from a more leisurely past. If they want reality they should attend the preparations for a village fete. Hysteria, jealousy, despair and ecstasy: the spectrum of human behaviour is manifest.

For the cub reporter carnivals and fetes are the summer substitutes for amateur dramatics and operatics.

In vigilant pursuit of stories I used to arrive in the morning — fetes are always held on wet Saturday afternoons — as the floats for the procession were assembling and the band was rehearsing before the pubs opened.

One Saturday morning when clouds were scudding in low from the sea I took the bus to a Norfolk village where the fete, or carnival, was to be held in a field recently occupied by a herd of cows.

The refreshment tent had just collapsed and beneath it was a hump which someone identified as the post-master. The lady chairman of the carnival committee dismissed his plight. "Just like old Bellamy," she said, as though old Bellamy grabbed every opportunity to secret himself beneath canvas.

The chairman, a Mrs. Bairnsforth, was indisputably in charge as, in fact, were all the women, anticipating by a couple of decades their ultimate emancipation. She was a formidable ginger-haired woman wearing slacks and sweater for the field-work.

"I trust you're going to give us a good write-up, Mr. Lambert," she said. "I don't really understand why they sent you — I normally do the write-ups." And then, suspiciously: "Aren't you a little early?"

"I'm always on the look-out for a good story," I replied as two men helped a bewildered post-master to his feet.

"It's all for charity, you know." A threat which most reporters in the/provinces encounter from time to time. "We don't want any bad publicity."

"No such thing," I muttered. A palpable lie which is exposed every day of the week.

She then threw in the most hoary threat of them all: "Your editor and I are great friends," and I determined from that moment to expose the slightest suspicion of corruption — coconuts glued to their pedestals, light-weight arrows at the darts-stall, under-age beauty queens.

I patrolled the field observing the preparations, making notes whenever I felt Mrs. Bairnsforth's gaze upon me. The refreshment tent had been re-assembled and lemonade, Tizer, pork pies and cheese sandwiches were stacked on a trestle table to be sold later at exorbitant profit.

A children's roundabout was being put together in one corner of the field; in another a coin-rolling stall from a fairground was being manipulated to reduce the chances of winning tuppence to about 1,000 to 1.

The band was half way through a selection from *Annie Get Your Gun* when a hoarse voice reached them from the lane leading to the field: "They're open, lads." The musicians streamed across the field leaving their instruments behind them.

Just then it was discovered that there were no wooden balls for the coconut shies; that the barrel organ imported specially from Norwich played only one tune to which some of the village stalwarts were already singing a ribald accompaniment;

that someone had opened the gate to the adjoining field and the cows were returning to their original pasture.

Two women, forgetting their independence, became hysterical as the cows, docile but inexorable, made their way across the field taking with them the bookstall and the second-hand clothes counter. "Do something," the women pleaded in between shrieks, "oh please do something."

Mrs. Bairnsforth was made of sterner stuff. Grabbing the stick on which old Bellamy, still dazed, had been leaning she stood in front of the cows and prodded the leader. It stopped for a moment, chewed the cud and stared at her through gentle, cartoon eyes; then it lowed deeply and magnificently and pushed her aside.

The situation was saved by a youth named Alf, the village simpleton; simple he might have been but some of the world's great inventions have been sheer, distilled simplicity. Alf opened the gate at the other end of the field and the cows filed out and were not seen again that day.

"You've got to hand it to young Alf," a carpenter named Gotobed (a common enough name in Norfolk) told me. "That's the way to the milking shed."

While helpers were searching for the wooden balls and installing a gramophone to supplement the barrel organ the common topic of conversation was the weather.

"Think it'll hold off?" nodding at the clouds drooping with rain.

"Might do."

"Didn't last year."

"Nor the year before neither."

What they meant was that they were praying for rain; that the afternoon would be a travesty of tradition if everyone wasn't drenched to the skin. The appearance of a patch of blue sky was greeted with as much alarm as meat in a vegetarian's stew.

In the lane outside, the carnival floats that would tour the village before the judging were jockeying for position. Some were splendid achievements — a handcart embroidered with flowers, a limousine converted into a submarine — but others lacked ingenuity: the baker's van showed no discernible difference from the baker's van that normally toured the district and a cardboard funnel did little for a farm tractor.

At midday Mrs. Bairnsforth announced through a foghorn that lunch would be taken. She and the other dignitaries were lunching at the vicarage; the rest of us were obliged to repair to the pub.

"And I want you all back here by one," she bellowed. "We're not finished yet, not by a long chalk."

"Silly old faggot," murmured Alf the simpleton.

In the pub, gleaming with horse brasses and copperware, the band was preparing itself for a strenuous afternoon. The drummer had bought a round and, as there were eight musicians, all fair-minded to a fault, a total of eight pints had to be sunk.

Old Bellamy was leaning on the bar with a medicinal glass of whisky in his hand; Alf ordered a fizzy lemonade because, he said, he wasn't quite himself in drink; Mr. Gotobed who had a jaw like a chisel and biceps like tennis balls bought me a pint of bitter. The four of us formed a unit, both convivial and defensive, in the way that it happens in English pubs.

Old Bellamy who was about thirty-five and a defeatist said: "I suppose you'll be putting that in your paper. You know, my humiliating experience."

I shook my head. "It wasn't exactly news."

He seemed disappointed.

Alf said: "Do you deliver the newspapers yourself?"

"Not really," I said. "I couldn't run round Norfolk and Suffolk in time."

"I've often wondered about that," he said.

Mr. Gotobed, a man of forthright expression, said: "Have you seen the crumpet?"

"You mean the entrants for the beauty queen contest?"

"The same. In most places they're chosen before the carnival. Not here. We choose 'em in the afternoon. You might get a story there, lad. There's been a bit of feeling in the village."

"Oh?" trying not to look too keen.

"Thirsty weather," said Mr. Gotobed.

"I bought him a pint and another lemonade for Alf.

One member of the band had brought his trombone into the bar and his colleagues were pouring beer into it. The trombonist blew into the mouthpiece and a jet of mild-and-bitter flew across the counter.

"Steady lads," said the landlord.

Mr. Gotobed sucked down half his pint and replaced his tankard on the counter. "It's the vicar's daughter," he said enigmatically.

"I beg your pardon?"

"Vicar's daughter's entered and there's them that don't think it's right."

"Ah." The first sniff of a story; the tingle that I was to experience for the rest of my journalistic career. "Have there been any protests?"

"Not overtly," he said. A surprising comment; perhaps he manipulated all conversation to a point where he could shake his head, wipe the foam from his lips and murmur: "Not overtly."

"But there's been a lot of talk?" I asked.

"Ah, that there has."

"Any possibility of any trouble this afternoon?"

"You'll just have to wait and see. Well worth the wait," flexing one bicep, "plenty of prime crumpet there."

131

From the field came the bellow of Mrs. Bairnsforth's voice through the hailer. "One o'clock. Come on, let's be having you."

We trooped back to the field, all except for the band who were now singing.

Mrs. Bairnsforth had changed into a bright silk dress which clung to her ample figure. The other women had also changed into their carnival finery. Above us the clouds drooped lower.

Villagers were now staggering into the field weighted with gifts for the bring-and-buy stall, books for the Carnival Library, fruit and vegetables and cakes. The lucky-dip was erected; two donkeys who were to give rides to the children were pulled into the field, a St. John's ambulance ominously arrived; the Boy Scouts who were to give a display of field-craft began fighting among themselves.

Alf was put in charge of the donkeys; old Bellamy was put in charge of a bucket of water — you dropped pennies into it in the hope of covering a sixpence at the bottom — where it was hoped he could come to no harm.

By 2.15 one crisis had arisen like a shark-fin above the others: the celebrity, a comedian from a sea-side show, who was to open the proceedings had not arrived. At previous carnivals the squire, a shy man who believed you could converse with flowers and spent much time chatting with his roses, had been coaxed reluctantly from his garden to perform the ceremony; but this year there had been an overwhelming vote in favour of recruiting a celebrity because, as Mr. Gotobed put it, "squire's as daft as a brush these days."

By 2.20 even Mrs. Bairnsforth showed signs of cracking up. From the pub she put in a phone call to the hotel where the comedian was staying. When she returned to the field followed by a group of lurching bandsmen she announced in the tone of a family doctor announcing a death: "Bad news I'm afraid, ladies. He forgot all about it."

But Mrs. Bairnsforth was a fighter. It was she and her kind who had held the Home Front together during the War. God help any German pilot who had parachuted into her back-garden. "Misfortune," she proclaimed, "was made to be over-come." And to Mr. Gotobed: "Go and fetch the squire."

Mr. Gotobed turned to me and grimaced. "Bloody marvel-lous, isn't it. The old idiot will think he's addressing a bed of petunias."

Prompt at 2.30 the squire, still in his gardening clothes, was led to the rostrum where he stood staring vacantly at the expectant faces below him.

"Any minute now," said Mr. Gotobed, "he'll spray them with insecticide."

The squire, elderly and as nervous as a sweating racehourse, smiled gently and said nothing. Then he took an abrupt step for-ward, prodded, I supposed, by Mrs. Bairnsforth. "I declare this green house open," he murmured."

A round of applause and the squire was led away as the villagers swooped on the bring-and-buy stall in search of valuables inadvertently deposited among the moulting fox-furs, beaded evening blouses, chipped crockery and burnt kitchenware.

While the band, glassy-eyed and dishevelled, played a selection of Strauss waltzes with a funereal beat, I sought out the vicar to obtain his views on his daughter's participation in the beauty contest.

But he turned out to be one of the modern-thinking clergy-men whose articles in parish magazines on anything from poli-tics to morals are fodder for freelances when news is thin on the ground. He was tousle-haired and pugnacious. He didn't see anything bizarre in a cleric's daughter displaying her charms to the public. Why should he? Perfectly natural and healthy, wasn't it? No, he hadn't heard any adverse comment in the village. If anyone harboured unclean thoughts they should take a cold bath.

The first squall of rain smote the carnival as the village beauties paraded past the four judges — a local artist, the schoolmaster, Mrs. Bairnsforth and a plumber who for some inscrutable reason had been recruited to replace the missing comedian.

Self-consciously, on tottering high-heels, they marched up and down as the rain toppled their bouffant hair and strea.ned down the liquid make-up on their legs. They were not the most beautiful girls in the world but they were comely enough. Such was their bravery, their defiance, their hope shining through the rain, that I ceased to hope that there would be scandal.

But there would be one, Mr. Gotobed assured me, if the vicar's daughter won. Observing some of the village matrons, arms classically akimbo, I could see his point. My mind was divided: I wanted her to win — she was sweetly pretty with heart-breaking legs; on the other hand I didn't want to see her humiliated.

After the parade the judges departed to the refreshment tent to confer.

With the arrival of the rain the atmosphere of the carnival picked up considerably. Half the band played a selection from *The Maid of the Mountains* while the other half attempted *Land of Hope and Glory*. Alf was chasing an errant donkey and old Bellamy who had knocked over the bucket of water was combing the grass for coins.

There was one more mild disturbance before the winner of the beauty contest was announced. Among the pile of books at the Carnival Library, most of them ringed by teacups and speckled with mildew, a young man with larded hair and cunning eyes discovered a pornographic volume published by the Olympia Press in Paris.

Not for him the furtive exit to devour the erotica under a greenwood tree. He held it aloft and shouted: "Here's a thing; and a very pretty thing. Who is the owner of this pretty thing?"

All the faces around me seemed guilty.

"Perhaps," bellowed the youth, "the owner's name is inside the book.

Somewhere in the field someone was sweating in the rain.

The youth opened the book. "No name but a couple of initials," he announced, pausing for effect. Finally: "F.G. Do we have any F.G.'s here?"

Everyone looked at Frederick Gotobed who seemed to enjoy the accolade of decadence. He grinned, spread wide his hands and whispered to me: "Nothing to do with me, matey. But let 'em have their fun."

The rain had begun to sluice down, turning the grass into mint-sauce, as Mrs Bairnsforth mounted the rostrum to announce the winner of the beauty contest. She waited under her umbrella, rain pasting her dress against her body, as the villagers gathered eagerly beneath her.

First — the baker's daughter.

"Like I told you, a nice bit of crumpet," whispered Mr. Gotobed.

The Bible-faced women sighed, their arms dropped to their sides. Mounted for the charge, they had been knocked from their saddles.

The vicar's daughter came second.

"Bloody fiddle," said a voice at the back of the crowd. "I think — "

But his voice was drowned by a round of applause for the runner-up. She curtsied gracefully, fully aware, I'm sure, that in the eyes of every male in the crowd she should have won; but the baleful combination of religion and politics had intervened. But why should she care? She had made her stand and, outside the dripping hedges of the field, an exciting world beckoned to a girl as pretty as she.

Later the floats, aptly-named, drove round the village in the rain. I noted the names of the winners, bade farewell to Mr. Gotobed, old Bellamy and Alf and, circumventing Mrs. Bairnsforth, made my way to the bus-stop.

On the top of the bus I tried to construct a story around the beauty contest; but it didn't really stand up; and, in any case, the EDP only wanted a couple of paragraphs. Back at the office inspiration struck: the comedian who had let them down. The story made five paragraphs.

It wasn't until the Monday, reading my story in print, that it struck me that Mrs. Bairnsforth's initials were F.G.

XIV

It was about the time of the fete that Elizabeth and I decided to put to the test the debateable theory that two can live as cheaply as one.

Encouraged by winning thirty pounds on the football pools we were married one warm June day at King's Lynn register office. Terry Hutson was best man; Frank Keeler and Francis Rose were witnesses. We adjourned to a pub for a bottle of champagne, then travelled by train to Battle in Sussex to stay in a gamekeeper's cottage in which Elizabeth had been evacuated during the war.

We walked and we cycled amid drowsing countryside clotted with rhododendron blossom; we drank cider in small tobacco-stained pubs; we blew our money and returned to King's Lynn ten days later.

Eagerly we bought the *Lynn News and Advertiser* to read the report of our marriage. But the printer's devil who had cast his spell on the Maxime cinema advertisements had reappeared: according to the report I had married the registrar.

We had not taken the precaution of finding new lodgings in Lynn and, for the first two nights, we stayed in a pub next to the parish church; then we moved to a modern house owned by a widow whom we mistakenly thought had taken a shine to us.

We believed that she sympathised with the late hours I was forced to keep; that she enjoyed my pre-breakfast singing; that breakages and burned saucepans provided her with an endearing insight into the life of newly-weds.

She disenchanted me one morning after I had blown up the geyser in the bathroom. I smiled at her, engagingly I thought, unaware that my face was black and my teeth and eyes glittered like a Kentucky minstrel's.

She turned to Elizabeth and said: "I want you and your lunatic husband out of here within a week."

We found another lodging house about two miles out of Lynn at Gaywood. An old red-brick cottage opposite green meadows where cows grazed deep in mist on swallow-swooping evenings and mushrooms sprouted overnight.

The cottage belonged to a Mr. and Mrs. Baldry; she was a deceptively frail old lady and he was a white-haired, gaitered countryman who sat screwed to a chair beside the fireplace grunting at us as we passed through on our way to the outside privy.

We occupied one bedroom and a dining room downstairs where, despite lack of funds, we ate enormously. Shoals of sweet-meated prawns, sides of ham sparkling with points of ice, gooseberries and strawberries and sharp-fleshed cooking apples from the garden . . . The whole setting with the meadows across the lane reminded me of an old print, and we ate in the old-fashioned style.

But the trouble with the two-can-live theory is that the two can very soon become three. When I realised that Elizabeth was pregnant I knew that I had to move on; that if I stayed in King's Lynn with a baby I might never move again; that in sixty years' time I might still be in the same cottage, rooted to Mr. Baldry's seat beside the fire.

If no national newspaper had the good sense to employ me then I would offer my services elsewhere. What I needed now was experience in a big city.

I fired off a dozen letters and once again I got one optimistic reply. I went for an interview and one month later I joined the staff of the *Star* in Sheffield.

* * *

The change was dramatic.

From small town to big city; from sugar beet to steel.

There was grit and sulphur in the air, smog in the sky, soot on the buildings and, at night, the furnaces burned holes in the darkness. The voices of the people were gritty, too, with sharp accents and terse endearments. It was all speed and metallic noise, tramcars rattling through the suburbs towards the city centre, factory sirens discharging men whose lives were forged with steel. It was so hard, so loud that the weekend peace of the hills outside the city was tangible.

Kemsley House which housed the *Sheffield Telegraph*, a morning paper, and the *Star*, a tabloid evening, stood in the centre of the city, a gaunt place encased in white tiles smudged with soot.

There were about twenty reporters and we clocked in and out like the men in the steel foundries. Our lives were orderly and organised, we were as meek as drugged mice and the man we feared more than damnation was the chief reporter, Ernest Taylor. There was an editor and a news editor, but we were barely aware of them: Ernest Taylor was our editor, foreman, warder.

A shortish man with muscle-padded shoulders, he wore blue pin-striped or grey chalk-striped suits, his wavy black hair was regimentally trimmed, his cheeks were as pinkly clean as a bar of Lifebuoy and his voice was forged in a foundary.

We faced him at our desks on the editorial floor like schoolboys. If we were five minutes late we were summoned to his desk.

"Tisn't good enough, Mr. Lambert." Always Mister. "If ah can travel umpteen bluidy miles and get here in time then you living down't road can get 'ere on't time, lad."

At lunch-time, after we had written our stories, we had to sit at our desks waiting for the imperious dismissal to the canteen.

"Mr. Lambert?"

"Yes, Mr. Taylor?"

A nod in the direction of the canteen.

When we handed in a story we had to stand beside his desk awaiting his judgement.

"Mr. Lambert?"

"Yes, Mr. Taylor?"

"What the bluidy hell's this, lad?" holding aloft my typewritten copy as though it were infected.

With savage slashes of his pencil he would erase a couple of paragraphs, shake his head wearily — and keep me waiting an extra five minutes before allowing me to go and eat.

In the canteen we ate sausages and mash, followed by college pudding, and washed down with mugs of sweet tea — sometimes half a pint of bitter in the Dove and Rainbow.

In the afternoon we had to ferret about for overnights. These are a particularly tedious type of story, as boring to write as they are to read. First editions of evening papers are printed early in the morning and there is little to put in them — weather, fires, yesterday's crime stories with rehashed intros — so the empty spaces have to be filled with unremarkable stories produced the previous day.

Ernest Taylor's life was ruled by overnights; and so were ours. Each of us specialised in a subject and from our contacts we were expected to extract stories. My specialisation was Sheffield University, a stony pasture because students with anything interesting to say were engrossed in their studies and I was left with the minutiae of the Students' Union.

The University was the least exciting of the specialisations entrusted to me as a punishment because, within a week of arriving at the *Star,* I had upset Ernest Taylor and confirmed his cynical view that most of us regarded Sheffield as a stepping stone to Fleet Street.

I had now turned my ambitions to editors of the northern editions of the national papers which were published in Manchester. And I didn't see why the brevity of my stay at the *Star* should interrupt my campaign.

Among my applications was a letter to the northern news editor of the *Daily Mail.* I must have overdone it a bit and given the impression that I was something of an ace with years of big city experience behind me.

One evening, after wandering fruitlessly round the campus all afternoon, I returned to the office and sat down at my desk. After a while I felt Ernest Taylor's gaze directed at me. I bowed my head and made a show of examining my notes.

"Mr Lambert?"

"Mr. Taylor?"

"Come 'ere a minute, lad."

He sat back in his chair, fingertips touching each other. "Any overnights, lad?"

"Nothing much today, Mr. Taylor."

In front of me were the sub-editors' tables, behind me the reporters watching keenly.

"Nowt?"

I shook my head.

"Not surprising I suppose."

"I've had a few promises — "

"From bluidy news editors?"

"I don't think I quite — "

A red line had appeared above his shirt collar. "Not surprising there's nowt at University because you've been too bluidy busy writing letters, eh, Mr. Lambert?"

He stood up and paced back and forth watched by the rest of the reporters who realised that I had perpetrated something worse than a mistake in the Master Cutler's initials.

I watched him with despair. So this was how it was to end, in the City of Steel, in classically tragic circumstances — a bairn on the way.

He swung round and faced me, hands clasped behind his back. Typewriters stopped tapping. "Northern news editor of *Daily Mail's* been on to me."

My lips began to twitch.

"How long have you been on't paper, lad?"

"About — "

"I make it five days," he interrupted. "Northern news editor of *Daily Mail* seems to have got idea that you've been here longer. Seems to have got the impression that you're something — " rage garbled his speech — "something of a big shot round here."

I didn't reply; there was nothing to say.

"So you don't intend to stay with us long, Mr. Lambert?"

"I hope to." The lie stood up and took a bow.

"Hope to? Hope to, Mr. Lambert? If you bluidy hope to then why are you writing to bluidy *Daily Mail*?"

There was no answer to that either.

He prodded me in the chest and said in a tense voice: "Go home, lad. Just go home and get out of my bluidy sight."

When I got home there was a letter waiting for me from the northern news editor of the *Daily Mail*. There were no vacancies.

* * *

We were a wildly assorted bunch on the *Star,* most of us heading for Fleet Street *the hard way,* a few — Keith Renshaw, now with the *Sunday Express,* Tony Carthew who graduated to ITN — arriving straight from university. Among the former were Steve Morris, Tony Waller, Tony Carter, Don Hardisty and Ernest Taylor's deputy, Clive Frith, a good, hard-news reporter who often shielded us from Ernest's wrath.

But we weren't particularly convivial. Most of us had married young, we were always broke and the wildest extravagance we could afford was a half pint or so in the Dove and Rainbow.

I don't know why journalists marry so young but they invariably do. Sadly this impetuosity is often followed in Fleet Street by divorce at an early age.

But there were no such casualties on the horizon in those green days. All we were concerned with was advancing our careers — and finding somewhere decent to live.

XV

Next to hiding a dead body the most difficult act of conceal-
ment is hiding a pregnancy from a landlady. They can spot
them within a couple of days of conception!

Our first home was a bedroom and sitting room, with use of
kitchen and bathroom, in a semi-detached at the top of a hill,
down which tramcars swayed and whined on gleaming ribbons
of steel.

These tramcars took me to the office where, as another pen-
ance, I was daily assigned the motoring court while Elizabeth
looked for a job and tried to conceal her expanding waistline.
The rent was two pounds and ten shillings a week and I was
earning five pounds a week plus twelve shillings and sixpence
for copy-taking on Saturday afternoons.

Within a couple of weeks the first landlady had assessed Elizabeth's condition and we were on the move again. We stayed
briefly in a bungalow filled with cats before the landlady diag-
nosed the pregnancy and, once again, I was consulting the
small ads in the *Star*.

Most landladies shook their heads as we stood on their doorsteps. No dogs, no coloureds, no babies.

We were saved by a couple of Yugoslavs who owned a cav-
enous Victorian house beside a bus stop in Montgomery Road.
For three pounds a week they rented us the top flat which was
almost self-contained except that we had to descend a flight of

stairs to share a lavatory and bathroom with some more Yugo-slav tenants.

The flat was Spartan but the house had character — cosmo-politan exchanges outside the lavatory, a Himalayan ascent up the stairs as we passed through a stratum of curry-laden air emanating from the first floor flat occupied by a Sikh and his family.

On Sundays we caught the bus into the country where the air cleaned the soot from our lungs, where larks plunged from high blue skies and breezes muffled the heather and we imagined we could see the sea. There was a future up here: one day I would sail the faraway oceans and report momentous events.

Next morning — motoring court.

By October Elizabeth was waddling and I had to lever her up the Himalayan foothills. At the end of October we bought a battered pram — the sort that you occasionally see simpletons pushing along a village street. It cost ten bob.

On November 7th Patrick Andrew was born in hospital. A few days later he was operated on for a hernia having first been baptised by the hospital chaplain. I was convinced he was going to die; but within a few weeks he was smiling fatly from his scrap-iron pram as we wheeled him through the grey frozen streets of the City of Steel.

* * *

My career now took a curious turn, precariously balanced between triumph and disaster.

One of the big steel companies invited reporters from the *Star* and *Telegraph* to tour their foundary, offering a prize of five pounds for the best account of the tour which would be published in their house magazine.

After the tour I returned to the flat and wrote my story while Patrick Andrew bawled in his second-hand cot. Snow flakes fluttered against the window, curry fumes crept under the door.

I wrote through the night, then re-read it the following day. It was like a schoolboy's account of his holiday. I re-wrote it while the baby yelled encouragement.

Next day I typed it at the office and submitted it without hope.

For the next couple of weeks my assignments alternated between motoring courts and inquests that were never destined for headlines; anything that smacked of news-worthiness was handed to one of the more stable members of the staff.

But those inquests taught me about the inequalities of life. Babies smothered by mothers in the depths of post-natal despair, old people dying alone — milk bottles outside the door the only indication that a life had ended, children with leaden lungs dying from pneumonia because harassed parents had ignored a cough, bundles of ragged humanity that had once been loved by someone found in the gutter with a bottle of methylated spirits.

The rich had obituaries: the poor had inquests.

Inquests were deeply depressing, motoring courts were a yawn that slowly inflated during the morning.

On one occasion I sat through a case in which a motorist was charged with driving without insurance. A serious enough offence but in detail as riveting as a telephone directory.

Half way through the case an office messenger arrived to inquire whether I had any copy to take back to the office. I shook my head; this particular case wouldn't merit a paragraph among the truss-ads.

The case reached its inevitable conclusion and I dawdled back to the office, with canteen lunch and the afternoon hunt for overnights ahead.

Ernest Taylor was standing beside his desk. "Where is it, Mr. Lambert?"

"Where's what, Mr. Taylor?"

"The insurance case. Bluidy good story," apprehension beginning to dawn on his face.

"Oh that," I said, apprehension beginning to dawn on mine. "There was nothing in it."

The familiar red line appeared above his collar. "You mean you haven't got a note?"

"It was the usual sort of thing," I said. My hands had become clammy, the old smallpox/chickenpox feeling. "Not worth a paragraph."

He sat down, one hand reaching for the spike. "Chairman said it was a good story," he said, holding the spike like a dagger.

"Which chairman?"

"Chairman of magistrates, that's which chairman."

Since when had we been influenced by magisterial opinion?

"I'm sorry," I said with faltering dignity, "but I disagree."

"You do, do you, Mr. Lambert?" pointing the spike. "Do you know who chairman was?"

I shook my head. Unless they had some horrendous deformity they all looked much the same to me.

He put down the spike. Punched one fist into the palm of the other. "Bluidy editor-in-chief, that's who bluidy chairman was, Mr. Lambert."

We stared at each other. I had never seen the editor-in-chief. How was I to know? I backed away preparing to collect my belongings and depart gracefully.

"Come here, Mr. Lambert."

I stepped forward again awaiting the thrust of the spike through my ribs.

He handed me an envelope.

I ripped it open. Inside was a letter and a cheque.

"You've won steelworks competition, Mr. Lambert. Bluidy 'eck, lad" — an almost beseeching expression on his face — "I've got to give thee a rise with left hand and fire thee with right. What shall I do?"

I made a helpless gesture.

Finally he stood up, stuck out his left hand and congratulated me saying: "I just don't know about you, lad. I just don't know," and departed to explain to the editor-in-chief why instead of an account of a motoring insurance case, Derek Lambert's contribution to the paper that day would be an account of a tour of a steel foundary.

* * *

My career with the *Star* now took a turn for the better as a result of my prize-winning contribution.

Ernest Taylor was jubilant that a member of the *Star* reporting team had won in face of competition from the *Telegraph* which was regarded — by the *Telegraph* staff — as a superior journal. I was taken off motoring courts and given assignments that were more features than news stories.

When a newspaper wants to revive circulation that's been flagging in certain areas it publishes what are called slip-editions; in other words, pages with stories relating specifically to that area are slipped in for a limited edition.

I was sent to outlying regions to write special features for these slip-editions. I spent a week at Barnsley nervously interviewing celebrities — nervously because this was the territory of Ernest Taylor who was a fanatical supporter of Barnsley Football Club and reported their vicissitudes for the BBC on Saturdays.

I was also allowed to cover the fringe aspects of big news stories, some of which were covered by local staff reporters of national papers such as Peggy Robinson, the much-feared Sheffield staffer of the *Daily Express*. I covered the remoter aspects of a murder; I interviewed the owner of a Rolls-Royce who was reluctant to discuss his automobile because he was a dustman by profession.

But still my overweaning ambition was to get to Fleet Street. So Fleet Street and Manchester editors and news editors were now bombarded with copies of my prize-winning essay.

With little effect. Instead of joining a national I went to school. The school was part of Kemsley newspapers' training scheme. Once a week a crowd of us, below a certain age and of varying degrees of ineptitude, gathered in a classroom to be taught local government, court procedure, sub-editing, typography, reporting techniques, newspaper ethics . . .

What do you do if a man being interviewed announces half way through the interview that it's all off the record? Should he not have made that clear at the beginning of the interview? And should not the reporter therefore be entitled to report what he had said previously? A moot point which we discussed endlessly and hilariously because these sessions with an erudite teacher given the thankless task of controlling a group of rumbustious young men in their early twenties were regarded more as respite in our routine than periods of improvement.

I suppose we learned a great deal, but at the time it seemed that there was more to be learned out in the field. For instance, when to produce a notebook.

An injudicious flourish of a notebook can wreck an interview or impromptu conference. A starlet may have hinted that she and the thrice-married star of the movie they have just made are slightly more than good friends. The interview with

149

the starlet angling for a major role is easy enough, but the interview with the thrice-married star now guiltily returning to his third wife to avoid more alimony is a much more delicate affair. Up comes a reporter with an enormous notebook which he folds back before licking his pencil and barking: "Could we have that again."

Freeze. The star envisages the notebook as an exhibit at his next divorce proceedings. He holds up a palsied hand, a PRO says, "Okay, guys, that's it." All because of a notebook.

The argument *for* producing a notebook is, of course, accuracy. And there are many interviews, particularly those with politicians with denial tendencies, in which a note must be taken. But in minor interviews, where the quotes are not of stunning importance, it isn't always necessary; succinct quotes lodge in the brain and can be written up afterwards. After all, the police do it.

For some inexplicable reason we also learned poetry at the school, but the spectacle of one of us who had entered journalism to record the hurly-burly of life reciting Wordsworth reduced the rest of us to schoolboy hysterics.

On one occasion a reporter was reciting *Ode to a Grecian Urn,* his voice exploding with squibs of laughter.

At the end of the recitation Jock Higgins, a humorous Scot from one of the district offices, shot up his hand.

The tutor looked at him warily. "Yes, Higgins?"

"This Grecian Urn, sir."

"What about it, Higgins?"

"Was he any relative to Urn Taylor, sir?"

After school we retired for half a pint — among our number Don Cameron who later graduated to whole pints in Fleet Street and now works on the news desk of the *Daily Mirror* — before dispersing to the smoky suburbs of the city.

The most valuable lessons we had learned related to typography and for a month I worked on the subs table. Sub-editing is, to the layman, the most mysterious and least applauded of journalistic accomplishments: it is, in fact, the most skilful.

The sub has to compose headlines in a particular type-face across an allotted number of columns; he has to calculate to a hairsbreadth how many letters will fit across a column; he has to instruct the printers what size type the various paragraphs of the story should be; he has to cut a rambling report to five column inches or even one paragraph; he has to insert sub-headings to break up the story.

And he has to check facts, improve grammar, re-write gibberish, find additional material — and drink his tea.

Speed is the sub's master and his pencil darts like a seamstress's needle.

But the public is not impressed. "I know one of the editors of the *News of the World*."

"Assistant editor, ma'am?"

"No. A sub-editor."

"Well, he's not exactly an editor."

"Well, what is he then?"

Followed by a dissertation on sub-editing while a vacant expression crosses the questioner's features.

I enjoyed my sub-editing, deriving almost as much satisfaction from seeing the subbed copy in the paper as I did from seeing my written word in print; but I hadn't come into this business to sit at a desk so I returned to reporting. Although Ernest Taylor viewed my return with rather less enthusiasm than I did.

XVI

My final calamity in Sheffield involved my old bugbear — football.

Kemsley newspapers were at that time inordinately proud of their walkie-talkies through which major events were reported. And there is nothing in the North more major than a cup tie.

We were carefully deployed that Saturday afternoon: reporters posted on the routes that would be taken by the exuberant fans, reporters inside and outside the ground.

I was chosen to relay the atmosphere inside. All that I was expected to do was to jabber a few last-minute words into the receiver before the sports reporters took over by telephone.

In the morning, as supporters poured into the city, Ernest Taylor held a briefing conducted with meticulous attention to detail, like one of those scenes in a movie when a police chief arranges a stake-out.

Football was Ernest's love, journalism his dedication. He regarded us sternly, but there was a cajoling note to his voice: "Don't let me down, lads."

And none of us would have done so deliberately because we respected Ernest in the way recruits respect their drill sergeant.

Some of the reporting was to be done from office cars with radio telephones. During rehearsals the cars were sent to various parts of the city to see if radio communication was sustained. It was.

Then the walkie-talkies were tested. You humped them on your back and wandered into the city where you muttered: "One, two, three, testing, testing, over and out" and waited for a reply.

The trick was not to attempt to hold a two-way conversation; you transmitted while back at HQ they received; they transmitted while, standing self-consciously watched by giggling urchins, you received.

It all worked smoothly enough. Ernest sighed with relief and we adjourned to the canteen like troops eating a last ration of bully-beef before going over the top.

Then we took to the streets.

In the environs of Sheffield Wednesday's ground, the car taking me to the gates was almost overturned by rattle-waving crowds.

At the gates I struggled out of the car with the walkie-talkie strapped to my back. All around me were fanatical faces with wind-polished cheeks and damp noses, programme-sellers, ticket-touts, police.

There was laughter on the air, and gritty coal-face humour.

"What's lad over there doing?" pointing at me. "On fatigues, luv? Six times round parade ground wit' full-pack?"

I tried to stand up straight but the walkie-talkie weighed me down as I pushed my way towards the gates like a deformed tramp looking for cigarette ends.

Finally I reached the entrance. "Got Press pass, lad?"

Desperately I searched my pockets. If I hadn't got the bloody thing I would collapse on the ground and let the crowd trample me to death. I found it.

Then I was inside the ground. A great bowl lined with baying humanity. Only five minutes left to kick-off.

I headed for the pitch where my appearance with the great pack on my back was greeted with howls of delight. Perhaps I was some sort of last-minute cabaret act.

To hell with them. I manipulated my machinery and muttered: "Derek Lambert here, one two three, testing, testing."

Back came Ernest Taylor's unmistakeable voice. "Can't hear you, Mr. Lambert. Are you there?"

"I'm inside the ground," I said. "Fantastic scenes. Crowds swaying like corn in the wind . . . police have ejected two trouble-makers . . . gates locked . . . pitch in beautiful condition as green as Ireland . . . "

"Are you there, Mr. Lambert?"

"Gates locked five minutes before kick off . . . police have ejected potential trouble-makers . . . wildly-cheering crowds estimated at — "

"Mr. Lambert, are you there?"

"Of course I'm here. I keep telling you — "

"Are you bluidy well there, Mr. Lambert?"

"I'm trying to tell you — "

"For God's sake, let's have copy, Mr. Lambert."

"Crowds packed in stadium beneath leaden skies — "

"Mr. Lambert, for pity's sake, lad, where are you?"

And it was then that I swore bitterly and vehemently and articulately.

"Come on, lad," said a voice beside me. "Show's over. Players are coming ont' pitch." An official led me and my walkie-talkie away.

Back at Kemsley House Ernest Taylor was surprisingly jovial. The other reporters had provided adequate colour; I couldn't be blamed because no one had anticipated that the high walls of the ground would block my transmission.

And it was not until later that evening that the foul language heard all over Sheffield and the surrounding districts that after-

154

noon was traced to me because, through some fluke in transmission, it had been picked up and relayed over radio and television.

XVII

Animals feature prominently in reporters' lives because the British public is generally more interested in their behaviour than the behaviour of humans. Witness Chi Chi and An An, the unmateable pandas, Goldie the fugitive eagle and Victor the doomed giraffe.

The *Daily Mirror* was acutely aware of its readers' passion for animals and founded much of its massive circulation on this. A loveable lady named Betty Tay wrote most of the stories and they were beautifully illustrated by such photographers as Freddie Read, George Greenwell and Tommy Lea.

Legend has it that cats were for a long period banned from the *Mirror*. This is reputed to have occurred because Cecil King, then chairman of the group, murmured to an executive: "I rather prefer dogs to cats, don't you." This was interpreted as a Royal decree that cats were OUT and for years only really sensational pussy stories were published in the *Mirror*.

One of the most unfortunate animal stories concerned the publication in another paper of a prize-winning bull. The bull, not unnaturally, was tremendously endowed. But it was decided that the sight of these massive parts might give lady readers the vapours so in the photograph the bull was emasculated.

The owner of the beast promptly sued for many thousands of pounds and I remember a lawyer, sent to lecture us at Sheffield about the pitfalls of libel, citing this case, and saying in all seriousness: "I assure you, gentlemen, this is not a cock and bull story."

In Sheffield we had our fair share of animal stories — cats wandering hundreds of miles to find their way home, dogs putting burglars to flight, horses saved from the knackers' yard . . .

The oddest animal story I covered concerned a four-year-old tortoiseshell cat named Kitty Clover, a black tom named Tim and a grey tom named Tom.

One September morning Tim ventured forth to meet Kitty Clover — and repel his rival Tom.

Twenty-four hours later Tim returned home no longer the tom he was. He had been doctored.

Tim's owner discovered who had arranged the operation and sued a neighbour for Tim's loss of manhood. She was awarded agreed damages of twenty pounds with five pounds costs.

The county court judge said that the defendant claimed that Tim's wailing had caused her sleepless nights. She realised she had acted "in a high-handed manner" and wanted to apologise.

Later the owner of the hapless Tim told me that she believed that the woman she had sued had mistaken Tim for the rival grey Tom. And she disclosed that, since Tim's unsolicited operation, all Kitty Clover's kittens had been grey.

The appeal of caged-bird, dog and cat shows was appreciated by the *Star,* although detailed results were left to the weekly newspapers.

Dog shows provided the best copy because the characters of dogs, with names from a canine Debretts, changed at the shows: at home they were tail-wagging sycophants as they were groomed for stardom: at the shows they became recalcitrant prima donnas.

They barked, they nipped, they stood like statues when required to walk, they took off like greyhounds when required to adopt statuesque poses.

They reduced their owners to grovelling wrecks, and they led them in the ways of deceit as, with pieces of meat furtively held in clenched fists, they tried to make them walk.

I was once involved innocently in the machinations of an ambitious dog-owner. It was fairly obvious to everyone that the Dog of the Show cup would be awarded to either a great shaggy Old English Sheepdog or a Red Setter.

It so happened that I had written a story about the Old English Sheepdog who had been enlisted in the hunt for a missing child. The sheepdog had found the child in the countryside, stood guard over it all night and, in the morning, led the search party to it.

The sheepdog was a hero and received due recognition in the Press. I wrote the story and we carried a picture of the sheepdog laughing and peering at the camera through curtains of fur.

During the morning of the show the owner of the Red Setter, a tall woman in tweeds, approached me and said conversationally: "I hear you wrote that story about the sheepdog."

I said I had.

"A beautifully-written piece, I thought."

"Thank you very much," grateful for any praise because little had come my way since the walkie-talkie episode.

"Do you think he'll win?"

"I wouldn't be surprised," I said, and then, to repay her praise: "But I reckon your Red Setter is in with a good chance."

"He's been very poorly."

158

He looked a glossy picture of health but I sympathised: "I'm sorry to hear it."

"Hurt himself chasing a cat."

"Ah."

"Does the sheepdog have any weakness like that?"

Although I had admired the sheepdog I had not been particularly interested in its personal habits, but some stray remark surfaced from my interview with its owners. The photographer and I had been warned not to take him near the rabbit-hutches at the end of the garden. "Sends him berserk," said his owner.

"Starts barking and then the rabbits start mating," said the owner's husband. In retrospect it seemed a curious reaction but at the time I had been too concerned with the sheepdog's heroic qualities to ponder on his aphrodisiac effect on rabbits.

I told the owner of the Red Setter that rabbits had a strange effect on the sheepdog.

Lunchtime came and went and, by mid-afternoon, the show was in its final stages; and it was now inevitable that the ultimate accolade would fall either on the Red Setter or the Old English Sheepdog.

Or it was inevitable until a rabbit suddenly appeared in the ring. It sat down, folded its ears in fright and peered around through pink eyes.

Whereupon the Old English Sheepdog broke loose from its leash and hurled itself towards the rabbit who, deprived of a doe with whom to frantically mate, pressed itself into the sand.

When the sheepdog reached the rabbit it stopped. Owners and dogs watched hypnotised. Pink tongue hanging out, the sheepdog peered closely at the rabbit. The sheepdog dribbled and panted. No one moved. Not even the rabbit who was paralysed with fear.

Then, very gently, the sheepdog nudged the rabbit with its

159

nose. After a few seconds' nudging the rabbit got the message and, closely followed by the sheepdog, loped back towards the ring of spectators — back to the herd to which any stray must be coaxed according to a sheepdog's instincts.

There was a spontaneous round of applause and, shortly afterwards, it was announced that the sheepdog had won the Dog of the Show award.

As I departed to write my story I met the owner of the Red Setter.

I smiled at her. "I only said rabbits had a strange effect on the sheepdog," I said. "I didn't say *what* effect."

She glared at me. "I really don't know what you're talking about."

"And I didn't tell you what effect the sheepdog has on rabbits. But just out of interest," I said to her retreating back, "he gets them at it."

* * *

A common overnight story was a golden wedding. Couples wrote in to say that they were celebrating fifty years of marriage and a reporter would be dispatched to interview them before the anniversary.

The environment of Sheffield seemed to favour long and happy marriages because, on average, we carried about one golden wedding report a week.

They were not the sort of interviews that would have sent Sefton Delmer or Noel Barber racing to the cable office but they helped to tilt the balance a little in a profession where one is too often observing the frailties of human nature.

In small back rooms they patted each other's hands and smiled at memories while, from picture-frames on piano and mantelpiece, the family looked on. There *he* was, in puttees and peaked cap, on leave from the trenches, there *she* was in straw hat and bows, dimpling a smile at the photographer, trying to forget that he would be away again in the morning. And, as they remembered, they were not old at all.

They served me tea and home-made cakes or, with a wink, a tot of whisky from a Christmas bottle. Sometimes, war apart, they had never been outside Sheffield, except for a weekend at Blackpool for the illuminations which still shone like a searchlight in their lives.

In terrace houses shouldering each other towards the foundries, stems of smoke fingering the smog, hollowed doorsteps scoured clean, they had shared half a century of domestic history — babies and bereavement, poverty and small riches — and it was all so much more important than the great follies that make the front pages.

The men wore boots with toe-caps like black mirrors, shirtsleeves hoisted around their biceps; they carried coughs in their lungs and scars from hot metal on their hands. The women wore print dresses, hair tied in buns, a little bowed from producing all those picture-framed babies who now had babies of their own.

Perhaps they had once planned to travel the world. To settle in Australia. But the first, war-weary footsteps back in 1918 had taken them only as far as this sooty patch. In any case it didn't matter because at this moment all they could remember was the sharing.

The interviews, however, were not always as cosy as this. I interviewed one couple who had lived in the same house ever since they were married. They had been through hard times together — the Depression, strikes, two sons lost in the Second World War.

He was a small man with an energy-sapping walrus moustache; she was on the plump side, placid with cheeks that had

161

no right to be so rosy in this sulphurous atmosphere.

They brought out their album; they brewed tea with a blackened kettle of water which they balanced on the fire; they held hands; just before I left he gave her a little peck on the cheek.

"When will it be in't paper?" they asked.

Always wary about this question, I said: "Probably in a couple of days but I can't promise anything."

They nodded understandingly: life had been full of disappointments. But they were stoic, after all they had each other.

The husband stayed in the sitting room stroking his moustache while his wife accompanied me to the front door.

She gripped my arm. "Are you married, lad?"

I nodded.

"Any little 'uns?"

"One."

She relinquished her grip. "Then there's nowt you can do about it."

"I'm not sure — "

"You're trapped, lad. When little 'uns come you're trapped."

"But you've had a happy marriage," I said.

"Aye." She nodded grimly. "Aye." She glanced behind her, gripped my arm again and hissed: "If I'd had a gun I'd 'ave shot the old bugger years ago."

XVIII

One late-summer day I was dispatched to a village which shall remain nameless because the crime allegedly perpetrated there was so heinous that it wouldn't be fair to subsequent generations who revere their parents and grandparents to identify it.

The information reached the *Star* in the form of a letter from an anonymous correspondent. Ernest Taylor handed me the letter shading his eyes as though the contents had seared his eyeballs. I understood his feelings — the correspondent claimed that a village cricket team had been cheating!

Details were sparse but the informant implied that the cheating was not merely an isolated incident provoked by overwhelming temptation: it had systematically been practised throughout the season in pursuit of an inter-village trophy. If a reporter liked to present himself at 6 pm in a pub in a neighbouring village everything, the correspondent hinted darkly, might be revealed. To identify himself the reporter should carry a copy of the *Star* in his right-hand jacket pocket.

I caught a bus to the village and ordered myself a half pint of bitter in the pub. Presently a woman with Eton-cropped hair wearing heather-mixture tweeds and brogues joined me at the bar and said: "Are you the man from the *Star*?"

I patted the newspaper in my pocket. "The very same," I murmured fatuously, thrown off balance by the appearance of a woman.

"Come out to the car," she said, "we'll be less conspicuous there." The car was an old green Riley which she drove at a majestically slow speed and it seemed to me that nothing could have been more conspicuous. She stopped in a lane, unbuttoned her jacket, lit a cigarette, inhaled with gusto and said: "I suppose you're surprised that I'm a woman."

As I wasn't totally convinced that she was, I smiled vaguely.

"It isn't entirely a man's world, you know. Is there any reason why a woman shouldn't be interested in cricket?"

I said there wasn't.

"And it takes a woman to spot a man's deceits."

"Ah," I said thankfully, "you're referring to the cheating."

"It's been going on all summer."

"What sort of form has it been taking?"

"I want you to see for yourself. Are you free this Saturday?"

I usually earned an extra twelve shillings and sixpence by taking sports copy on Saturday but I had no doubt that Ernest Taylor would arrange for my release to disprove this slur on the name of Yorkshire cricket.

"I expect so," I told her through the fog of cigarette smoke.

"You mustn't approach me."

"Will you be among the spectators?"

"I shall be in the pavilion young man. I'm the official scorer, you see."

"For — ?" naming the team under investigation.

"Certainly not." She told me that she was the scorer for the village where we had met. A glimmer of light.

"And you're playing — on Saturday?"

"In the final."

I opened the window to release some of the smoke while she lit another cigarette from her butt. Had she any proof?

"Only what I've seen with my own eyes."

"I don't see . . ."

"I'll tell you what to look out for."

She took a red notebook from the glove compartment and ran a tobacco-stained finger down the pages. There were six definitive accusations and a few dark suspicions.

The most serious allegation concerned the twelfth man. According to my informant he was stationed among the spectators near the sightscreen armed with a mirror; when a batsman was about to strike the ball he was blinded by a flash of sunlight.

Umpires, she claimed, had been got at with promises of gifts of poultry at Christmas; pitches had been doctored; professional cricketers had been brought into the side at the last moment; visiting teams had been given spiked drinks at lunchtime; gamesmanship was rife.

"What sort of gamesmanship?"

"You know the sort of thing. Standing back when you're batting when the bowler's half way through his run. Appealing for everything to upset a batsman's concentration. And singing," she added.

"Singing?"

"One of their slips is always singing. Not loudly. Just humming."

A singing cricket team. Perhaps there were possibilities there. A music-hall act like the singing barbers of Chicago.

"What does he hum?" I asked. *"My defences are down?"*

"Apparently it's mostly church music."

"But can't the umpire do anything about it?"

"The square-leg umpire can't hear it," she explained. "Whenever there's a complaint the culprit denies it."

The Curious Case of the Singing Slip. "Watson, book me on the 11.55 sleeper."

"They should record it," I suggested.

"I hadn't thought of that," at which stage I wondered if she was completely cracked.

"I don't see how I can prove any of this," I told her.

"You don't believe me, do you?" The first sign of vulnerability.

"I didn't say that. But there would have to be some public denunciation before I could write anything."

The notion was appealing. A conventional poker-school cheating scene transferred to rural Yorkshire. Six-shooters brandished over the cucumber sandwiches.

"Are you suggesting that I denounce them?"

"It would help the story."

She lit another cigarette. "They wouldn't believe a woman."

"Well," I said, "it's up to you. But I'll come along anyway."

When I reported back to Ernest Taylor he looked at me appealingly. "A load of codswallop, Mr. Lambert?"

"I don't know." I gave him the details, pausing to let him groan when I mentioned the singing slip.

"Is she bonkers, Mr. Lambert?"

I shrugged. "I wouldn't like to pass an opinion."

He sighed. "Well you'd best go there on Saturday and clear it up once and for all."

It was a perfect late-summer day; the sky dark blue, trees dusty and languid, the sound of a harvester throbbing through the valley.

A refreshment tent had been put up beside the pavilion and tattered bunting looped through the hawthorn trees encircling the ground. Wooden benches, already occupied by old men, edged the boundary: the nobs had brought their own deck-chairs. The church clock, said to have been damaged by a stray bomb during the war, chimed three every hour, the hands of the clock above the wooden pavilion hadn't moved for twenty years — so perfectly timeless an atmosphere that I wouldn't have been surprised to see W.G. Grace stride out to the wicket.

I stationed myself beside the small terrace in front of the pavilion where the teams' families and girl-friends sat, having previously tried to spot the cads, the bounders, the cricket-sharps, in the village pub at lunch-time.

The prime suspect, of course, was the home-team's captain, a big beery man with a thatch of whiskers who owned a small steel foundry; I searched his face for any stain of dishonesty but his eyes, peering from between flamboyant eyebrows and swaggering moustaches, were as clear and bright as the steel he forged.

Number two suspect had to be the twelfth man who was supposed to blind batsmen with barbs of sunlight. Where was the little ferret?

"You might get a bat today, George," said a man in a striped blazer pouring beer down his throat from a pewter tankard. "Alf Wheeler's feeling a mite queezy."

Ah, George the twelfth man. I consulted the list of fifteen possible players supplied by my informant. There was only one George. And he was a bank manager.

From behind my half-pint pot I surveyed the rest of the players. The wicket-keeper who kept bending at the knees as though the bar was the stumps; an aged spin bowler named Muggeridge who had tricked arrogant batsmen for thirty years or more; a willowy youth straight from his school eleven; a chunky middle-of-the-order batsman said to have played for Yorkshire second; a couple of aloof young men who doubtless played with style. They were the only members of the team in the pub; perhaps the remainder were conspiring at this very moment.

The home team won the toss and elected to bat. At the open

window of the pavilion sat my informant with her green-ruled score book in front of her, pencil in one hand, cigarette in the other.

A young fast bowler in whom Yorkshire talent scouts were said to be interested opened the bowling, pounding down the slope from the church end with oiled, athletic grace. The delivery was short and the home team's bewhiskered captain hooked it contemptuously for six. The next ball brushed his moustache and hurtled past the wicket-keeper for four. At this rate there wouldn't be any cause for cheating and Ernest Taylor would be a happy man.

The captain received the next delivery in the crotch and fell to the ground. When he had recovered he took an enraged swipe at the next ball which reached the boundary in one bounce shattering the windscreen of a parked car. He blocked the next and gave a gentle return catch to the bowler off the last ball of the over. Fourteen for one.

One of the young stylists now faced a lanky bowler with an erratic windmill action. The first ball, released with alarming velocity from one of his flailing arms — you couldn't be certain which — flew straight into the wicket-keeper's gloves, while the young stylist walked down the pitch to prod a rebellious blade of grass. The next ball which happened to leave the bowler's arm at full stretch shattered the stumps. Fourteen for two; perhaps we might soon see some skullduggery.

The former Yorkshire second-eleven player was sent in to retrieve the situation. This he dourly did and, with the assistance of the schoolboy, the score moved at a funereal pace to fifty. Then a slow bowler with a suspect round-arm action was brought on and took two wickets in his first over. Fifty for four.

The second young stylist came in. The slow bowler's first ball hit him on the pad and all the fielders invoked the heavens to give him out: the umpire didn't. A turkey for the umpire on Christmas Eve?

But apart from that — the umpire later said the batsman had played the ball on to his pad — there were no apparent cases of sharp practice, although one batsman did stand away from his wicket causing the windmill to pull up short, arms whirling impotently.

They were all out for 145 just before tea, a respectable total but a beatable one. Now would be the time for foul play, the hour of the singing slip.

Around me flasks of tea were being opened, sandwiches unwrapped. Small boys bowled and batted in the outfield while swallows skimmed the grass between them. Far away, above the moors, I heard the first rumble of thunder.

The young Yorkshire prospect who had opened the bowling in the first innings was out first ball to the schoolboy who seemed more of a prospect. No call for any flash practices beside the sightscreen yet.

Another wicket fell with ten runs on the primitive scoreboard. Then their captain, wearing an orange and yellow cap, trousers held up with an orange and yellow tie around his vast stomach, was joined by their wicket-keeper built in the mould of Godfrey Evans. And he batted like Godfrey Evans saving England from humiliation.

Sixty for two. Seventy for two. They drove and hooked and cut as though they were wielding scimitars. I looked around for the home team's twelfth man, the bank manager, who had not been called upon to play, Alf Wheeler having overcome his queeziness. I listened in vain for the singing slip who was either the hirsute captain or a sulky looking lad who had scored a sulky three. I spotted the bank manager strolling thoughtfully in the direction of the sightscreen.

"Follow me, Watson." He reached the sightscreen as the

wicket-keeper lofted a six over the pavilion and the church clock struck three.

I stood behind the bank manager as the wicket-keeper faced Muggeridge whose wiles were no match for unbridled arrogance this gasping day.

The wicket-keeper played the next ball defensively. Then Muggeridge elected to bowl round the wicket. The bank manager slipped his hand into the inside pocket of his blue blazer, resplendent with a military badge, as the first fat drop of rain fell.

The wicket-keeper glanced the ball for two. The bank-manager's body seemed to tense. Then lightning forked the sky which had suddenly darkened from blue to bruised grey. A fitting atmosphere for the odious act which might be enacted in front of me — except that the theatrical effects defeated the plot.

These were no distilled drops of heat: this was the end of the summer. The clouds burst and the cricket field became the bed of a cataract. Drenched within a second the players, led by Muggeridge, raced for the pavilion as thunder cracked, trees bent and the dust-patches at the wickets turned to mud.

The game was abandoned and I don't know to this day whether the bank manager was reaching for a mirror, a gun or a cigarette case. Or whether one of the two slips had launched into Handel's *Messiah* as Muggeridge prepared to bowl that ball that was never delivered.

XIX

Throughout this period letters rejecting my applications for jobs dropped through the letterbox beside exotic envelopes for the Sikhs and Yugoslavs.

My envelopes were always of good quality, neatly typed, sometimes embossed with the name of the newspaper. *The Times, Manchester Guardian, Daily Telegraph, Scotsman, Yorkshire Post:* class papers were given every opportunity to avail themselves of my talents along with the popular papers, *Express, Mirror, Mail, Herald, Graphic* and *News Chronicle.*

My mail was also swelled by rejection slips from various magazines to which I had sent articles. *The Strand, Everybodys, John Bull, Argosy, Lilliput, Answers, Tit-Bits.* Occasionally some kindly reader would scrawl "Shows promise, not quite our style" on a rejection slip and I would swagger to work bound for the Algonquin to meet Dorothy Parker rather than the Dove and Rainbow to escape Ernest Taylor.

Half way through my sojourn in Sheffield I decided to give the BBC a trial. I devised a series about a penniless young couple from the South eking out an existence in an attic flat in the North.

And there one morning lying on the door-mat was a BBC envelope so small that it couldn't have contained the rejected outline of my series.

As I climbed the stairs through the curry-belt I slowly eased open the evelope.

Two paragraphs. Perhaps I would be good enough to visit a BBC executive in Manchester. Could I telephone his secretary and make an appointment.

My stomach joined in the excitement and I couldn't eat any breakfast. Ideas for the series surfaced like fish nibbling bread.

While Elizabeth fed the baby we stared across the grey rooftops into the future. First the publicity interviews in which we would be identified as the couple in the series. Television appearances — we didn't actually know anyone wealthy enough to own a TV — invitations to write for the national Press (that would teach them), a house, perhaps even a car . . .

During my lunch break I walked to a telephone box as far away as possible from Kemsley House in case Ernest Taylor had installed bugging devices in all the nearby kiosks.

The switchboard put me through to the executive's office. A girl with a cool voice answered. *"Mr. Lambert?* Ah, let me see now." The sound of rustling paper as she searched a desk to find out who I was. "Ah yes, Mr. Lambert. Thank you so much for telephoning us."

Silence.

"Are you still there, Mr. Lambert?"

"Yes," I said, in a strange guttural voice that didn't sound like mine, "I'm still here."

"Well, when do you think you could come and see us?"

"Would next Wednesday be all right?"

"Yes, that will be fine. How would three o'clock suit you?"

"That would be fine."

"Very well, Mr. Lambert, then we shall expect to see you next Wednesday at 3 pm."

Click.

I walked back to Kemsley House wondering about the strange voice that had issued from my mouth. Some complex

172

associated with the BBC, I decided.

Next Wednesday Elizabeth telephoned Ernest Taylor and said I was in bed with a feverish cold. I caught the train to Manchester huddled in my overcoat like some theatrical crook in case anyone spotted me.

It was raining as the train nosed through the shining wet suburbs of Manchester. It should have been depressing but, in fact, it was exhilarating watching through yellowish, rain-spattered windows as streets of houses rotated as though on an axis.

I lunched at a Lyons tea-shop. Vegetable hot-pot in a brown china bowl, individual apple pie and the best coffee which I, in my limited experience, had ever tasted.

At 3 o'clock I presented myself, aware that my lunch was beginning to grumble and whine.

"Ah, Mr. Lambert." He stood up and shook my cold, wet hand. "Please take a seat," sitting down himself and picking up my manuscript so that, from the back, I could see the thin patches where I had used a rubber. "Mmmmm." The unbound manuscript looked a poor thing beside the other manuscripts professionally typed and bound on his desk. "Mmmmm."

He peered at me over the top of my manuscript — a youngish man with oiled hair worn in a slight quiff, wearing a dark green suit. I thought he would have looked more at home at the Hammersmith Palais.

"Your first attempt?" he asked.

"Yes."

"Mmmm. Not a bad idea. Not a bad idea at all." As if this was the first time he had looked at it. "Of course we would want to see a lot more to make sure you could sustain the idea."

"Of course," I said.

"Would you envisage writing the scripts yourself?"

"I'd have a bash," I said incongruously.

"Mmmmmm."

"Well, I tell you what, I'll consult with some of my superiors and let you know."

"Mmmmmm," I said.

"How would that suit you?"

"Can't you let me have a more definite answer now?" I asked.

He shook his head. "I'm not authorised to take such a decision by myself."

"I see," I said.

He rose to his feet, as though about to ask me to dance, stuck out his hand again and said: "Not a bad idea. Not a bad idea at all."

Perhaps it wasn't. But I was never to know. I telephoned twice to see if his superiors had come to any decision and, on each occasion, was fobbed off with some diplomatic evasion. Pride prevented me from telephoning again. About nine months later I received a bulky envelope with my manuscript and an apologetic note inside. The manuscript, said the writer, had been found in the back of a drawer and they were returning it because the executive who had been handling it had long since left.

To take a job with Mecca dance-halls probably.

* * *

Meanwhile domestic life continued its impoverished course.

An outing these days was a Sunday walk to a park pushing the old pram like a husband and wife in the rag-and-bone business, with occasional alarms when a wheel broke loose and rolled into the gutter. Inside the pram the smile of Patrick Andrew grew wider as his face grew fatter.

Occasionally we visited the homes of other reporters and their families, all as hard-up as ourselves. Beer (whisky was for

174

rakes and exploiters of sweated labour) and sausages was the fare; occasionally they came to us, mouths watering as they smelled the curry, hiding their disappointment when the inevitable sausages were served.

The attic flat was well suited to parties because there was little you could damage. Only once did we threaten anything more serious than cigarette burns and broken windows and that was when the frying pan, in which Elizabeth was cooking the evening meal, caught fire and I managed to extinguish the flames with a cushion from the sofa which we subsequently turned upside down to hide the scars.

But we lived well in our cabin above the bus-stop. Great big cook-ups, macaroni cheeses, bubble-and-squeak, Sunday brunches. Every evening I sat tapping out articles and short stories on a Heath-Robinson typewriter that had three levels of type so that, if you forgot to depress the key for the third pressure, you typed capital letters instead of exclamation or question marks. Letters of application, features, short stories for *Argosy,* an entry for the *Observer* essay competition . . . they were all composed on this antique machine.

Nappies steamed around the fire — I had to lug buckets of coal up the stairs from a verminous cellar — the baby slept by day and woke tumultuously at night, and in the bedroom we kept what the Americans call a honeybucket which had to be surreptitiously emptied before the Yugoslavs reached the lavatory in the morning.

Despite these unromantic circumstances I submitted several romances to *Woman* and *Woman's Own.* But I suspect that a whiff of steaming nappies or honeybucket infiltrated into the envelopes because they were all rejected.

If two could live as cheaply as one, two-and-a-half certainly could not. We bought clothes at second-hand shops, we gratefully accepted babies' clothes from the mothers of children who had outgrown them, we never took a bus when we could walk. Our most frequent expenditure seemed to be gripe water which I ladled down the baby's throat at 2 am.

In the morning Elizabeth would keep watch at the window while I shovelled down bacon and eggs. When she spotted the bus in the distance she would shout to me and down the stairs I would charge, dodging a Yugoslav with a distended bladder, and bounding across the garden to hurl myself on to the running board of the bus, toast and marmalade in hand.

All in all it would have been difficult to find an existence further removed from the slick newspaper world projected by Hollywood. But the *Star* had introduced me for the first time to the full complement of a big editorial floor. Reporters, subs, photographers, retouchers, wire room operators, copy boys, copy-takers . . .

Although the frantic scramble which the public expects was rarely apparent, nonetheless it was there — but in the brain, in typing fingers and scribbling pencils; the speed was in decision, inventiveness, transmission.

The most formidable men I met were the photographers. I had worked with Claud Fisher but, beautiful cameraman that he was, he was not one for belting off a picture of a bank robber struggling with the police, rushing it to a wire machine and transmitting it to head office.

News photographers have always adopted a somewhat derisive attitude towards reporters, treating them as a rather effete bunch, an attitude which is rooted in the knowledge that, if they miss a picture, the loss is irrevocable whereas a reporter can saunter up and complete his work after the event.

They are hard-bitten and clannish and their temperament is compounded of the necessities of their job: Herculean patience during a long, door-stepping vigil while they assess speed and aperture in the fading light, and mercurial reflexes as a camera-shy subject tries to make a bolt for it.

They are not happily disposed towards reporters who manage to get between camera and subject; they have been known to hold forth at great lengths about journalists who report some phenomenon they haven't photographed.

The first *Star* photographer who accompanied me on a story was in his late fifties, grey-haired and laconic. He had seen young reporters come, he had seen 'em go. In his time he had covered everything from Brownie outings to mass murders.

And he had a car which made me feel even more inadequate. Photographers, who always seem to acquire cars before reporters, are justifiably resentful about acting as chauffeurs.

This photographer only became human when he recalled the old days of cameramen using flash powder instead of bulbs. His favourite story concerned a photographer who spent an hour setting up a tableau on the stage of a village hall. At last it was arranged to his satisfaction and the fatigued participants posed for the last time, stomachs sucked in, smiles adjusted. The flash powder ignited and burned down the hall. This made the photographer laugh helplessly.

My own favourite story about photographers concerned a diminutive cameraman with a bald head who, at some lavish ball, found himself dancing with the film star, Jane Russell.

Jane Russell was renowned for her magnificent chest. For the tiny photographer skipping round the ballroom this became an eyeball-to-bosom confrontation.

It was all too much. Suddenly overcome by the proximity of these superb mammaries he stuck his bald head in between them and shook it from side to side like a terrier shaking a rat.

A member of Miss Russell's entourage noticed the incident and complained to the photographer's editor. He was promptly sacked. But, on hearing of his dismissal, Miss Russell phoned the editor and pleaded for leniency on the grounds of irresistible temptation. The photographer was reinstated.

The occasion of this, my first story with a *Star* cameraman, was an old lady's one hundredth birthday. He had to photograph the centenarian holding her telegram of congratulations from the new Queen and, throughout the journey into the snow-patched hills, he complained that he had been taking the same picture for the past twenty-five years.

When we arrived at a flintstone cottage brushed by low clouds the family had gathered, generations of them. They spilled out of the cottage on to the porch where their breath turned to frost and their feet ground the ice to powder.

"Better get picture of cottage," said a grandson. "Born and bred here, she was. Never left it as far as I know. Did she, Alf?" turning to an identical grandson.

There is nothing more calculated to infuriate a photographer than advice on where he should aim his camera. The *Star* cameraman ignored the grandson and shouldered his way inside the cottage.

The centenarian's sons were old men and they sat around on the few available chairs, a little put out that anyone could be older than them. They wore serge suits that hung loosely on them, waistcoats and watchchains, ties with knots as tight as brussel sprouts lanced with gold tie-pins; they all looked naked without their cloth caps. Each smoked a pipe, each supped from a bottle of brown ale.

Grandsons and daughters were middle-aged, a worried-looking lot wearing clothes that crackled; great-grandsons and daughters looked younger but not much. I gave up trying to calculate the relationship of teenagers and floundering babies to the old lady.

Snapping-gummed and wicked-eyed, she held court, issuing commands, sipping cooking sherry, surveying her issue, unsparing with the hypocrites. "Hetty? Fancy seeing thee. Twenty years, isn't it? Come for sherry, have you?"

She looked a bit like Queen Victoria.

I approached her hesitantly, ashamed of the question perched on my lips. "To what do you owe your longevity?" How many centenarians had been asked that?

"To what do I owe what, lad?" she asked.

My lips began to twitch. "Why do you think you've lived so long?"

The wicked eyes surveyed me. She and I both knew it was a daft question. She sipped her sherry. "What does thou think, lad?"

This wasn't the way interviews were conducted in the correspondence course.

"I don't know," I said desperately. "Clean living . . . maybe your diet . . ?"

"Clean living be blowed." She stuck out her empty glass. "Fill it up, lad." I filled it up and gave it back to her. "So thou wants to know why I've lived to be hundred, eh? Well I'll tell thee."

At that moment the photographer let off a flash. It stopped her in mid-speech and made the babies cry. Then the familiar hunting cry of the cameraman — "Just one more." Another flash. "And now one with telegram." The telegram was thrust into the old lady's hand and another flash blindingly lit the room; in a corner a dog began to bark.

The old lady seemed umperturbed. "You listen, lad, and put it down in thy notebook. Where is it?" staring suspiciously at me. "Thou didst say thou was from't *Star,* didn't thou?"

So much for the notebook theory. I produced my pad, licked my pencil like a tradesman taking an order.

"Anyone who thinks clean living makes thee grow old wants head examined. Hast thou got that?"

I said I had.

"And doest thou know why?"

I shook my head.

"Because when't people say *clean* living they doesn't mean it. They mean unnatural living, that's what they mean." She leaned forward conspiratorially. "When I was a girl I lived it up, lad, aye that I did. None of this fancy dieting. I was courted by every lad in't village — good looking ones, any road — and I led 'em a merry dance I can tell thee."

"So your recipe for longev . . . for long-life is to live it up?"

"To live it to full, lad. Take what thou's been given and enjoy it, don't ration it."

"I'm told," I said, "that you've never left this village. Is that true?"

"I went ter Sheffield once," she said. "Couldn't stand it. Couldn't breathe."

"Apart from that you've never left the village?"

"Never. Why should I? Take look out of window, lad, and you'll see why. Hills and sky, different every hour of day. This is my world: I've never wanted to know owt 'other."

I closed my notebook with a snap. "Thank you very much — and a very, very happy birthday."

"Aye," she said, "but I won't if thou doesn't get me another glass of sherry." She leaned closer. "A big 'un this time."

As we drove back through falling snow the photographer grumbled: "Same bloody picture every time."

I saw him later outside Kemsley House heading for his car. "Coming for one at the Dove and Rainbow?" I asked.

He scowled. "I've got to go back to see the old girl," he added. He held up his hand to fend off questions. "Something wrong with camera — none of the pictures came out."

And off he went to take same picture yet again.

XX

My first publication in a national Sunday newspaper was an accident.

My sister, an exuberant blonde eleven years older than myself, who had tried her hand at jobs ranging from barmaid to book-keeper, was at the time in a culinary frame of mind.

She had cooked at Eton, and she had cooked at one of those schools where pupils go unpunished and are allowed to express themselves freely; but, tiring of children throwing kitchen utensils at her, she had given in her notice.

Now she had applied for a job cooking for girl sea rangers on a boat moored in the Dart. Her chances were promising but there was one obstacle to be overcome: the housing of her miniature long-haired dachshund.

Animals were not permitted on board so my sister devised a brilliant compromise: she would build a houseboat, or a kennel-boat, for the dog and it would be moored alongside the girls' boat.

I heard all about this when visiting my parents from Sheffield. It seemed a good story, so I wrote it. At the same time I received a letter from the *People*, the Sunday newspaper, inviting me to London for an interview. What better example of my dashing, Fleet Street style than the dachshund story?

When I arrived in Fleet Street I went straight to the *People* offices where I was interviewed by an editorial executive who implied that my letter of application had somewhat over-stated my qualifications. Could I produce any evidence to support my dizzy claims?

Out came the typewritten story about the kennelboat. He nodded approvingly. "We'll let you know," he murmured. *Don't ring me, I'll ring you.*

It wasn't until I got back to the attic in Sheffield that I realised that I had left the story about the dachshund on the desk at the *People* office.

The following Sunday the story appeared in the paper. Two days later my sister was told that the cook's job was no longer available. Three days later I received a letter telling me that I wasn't sufficiently experienced yet for a job on the *People.*

A few weeks later I received a cheque for two pounds for the story.

But at least I had achieved an exclusive in a mass-circulation Sunday paper even if it had subsequently been overtaken by events. It represented a landmark and I sensed that I was about to make a breakthrough.

I was relieved of my university chores, motoring courts were a tedious memory. I was even given another rise — ten shillings a week.

Winter thawed, daffodils lit mud-grey gardens with saffron lights. There was a fresh urgency in the air and, above the smog, we sensed there were blue skies.

Intoxicated with the spring promise that reached our attic I fired off a fresh salvo of letters to Manchester. A few days later a letter arrived inviting me to go and see Jack Clarke, northern news editor of the *Daily Mirror.*

He terrified me. Sleek black hair, thinning a little, sharp-suited, brash and quick, he was to my mind the archetypal national newspaperman. He appraised me in my Chaplinesque flannel trousers and blazer on which the elbows shone brighter than the buttons; he made a few notes on a pad. God knows what they said. *Could do with a wash and brush-up.*

He picked up a copy of a northern edition of the *Mirror*, pointed at a story by a staffman and said: "What do you think of that?"

I examined it. My brain seized up. I read the first paragraph three times without understanding it. But it seemed competent enough.

"Well?" he barked.

"Punchy," I said.

"What?"

"Punchy. A good punchy intro."

"I think it's bloody awful," he said.

Silence.

"Well," he said, leaning back in his chair, feet on his desk, "I'll let you know."

I walked out of the *Mirror* office — a nondescript place in Hardman-street in those days — and walked past the *Mail* office on the corner of Deansgate. But it was such a beautiful day, so full of hope, that I didn't feel too depressed: something had to happen soon: it was written on the gentle breeze.

Two days later two letters dropped on the mat. One offered me holiday relief work on Reuters, the news agency, the other, from Jack Clarke, offered me holiday relief on the *Mirror*.

After three years of trying I had been offered two jobs on the same day. True it was only holiday relief, a precarious proposition when you're broke with a wife and baby to support. But such chances have to be grabbed before other ambitious young men intercept them.

As my shorthand was still more of a chase than a sprint, I decided that I wasn't agency material. Before leaving for work that morning I wrote a letter accepting the *Mirror* offer and, to clinch it, telephoned Jack Clarke later that day.

Ernest Taylor was philosophical when I handed in my notice. He stood up, hands clasped behind his broad back. "Aye, lad, well I knew you'd be off some day." He nodded towards the rest of his reporters. "Half of them will be gone before year's out."

He reminded me at that moment of a schoolmaster who instills the quintessence of his learning into a class of scholars, only to see them depart every summer, enrichened and already forgetting. He had been a very good tutor, had Ernest Taylor.

Elizabeth and the baby were going to her home in Dartford in Kent, while I looked for accommodation in Manchester. For the last time we passed through the curry-belt carrying battered suitcases and the baby in a carry-cot.

After seeing them off on a train I went for the last time to the Dove and Rainbow for a halves-of-bitter farewell.

Ernest Taylor was there. He bought me a beer, shook my hand and said: "Good luck, Mr. Lambert," and with that familiar shake of his head: "Bluidy 'eck, lad, I never knew about you," and was gone.

* * *

A few days later I reported to the *Mirror* office in Manchester, arriving at the same time as another holiday relief, Bernard Shrimsley, who was later to become editor of the *Sun* and the *News of the World*.

I was to become editor of nothing. But at least, after so many faltering footsteps, it seemed as if I had taken a stride in the direction of Fleet Street.

XXI

I had three months in which to prove myself. Three months in a league, as different from my previous experience as baseball from rounders, in the company of a band of slick, experienced newspapermen who had clawed their way up from the weeklies.

The mood of the office was set by the news editor, Jack Clarke, who was that rare personality, the newspaperman as envisaged by the public. Fast-talking, fast-moving, as canny as a private-eye and as hard as Blackpool rock. And that was how you had to be on the *Mirror* in those days when firing was as common as hiring.

His second-in-command was Roly Watkins, a man of gentle charm which belied singleness of purpose equal to Jack Clarke's; this was later recognised when he was made news editor in London.

But it was the reporters who were more intimidating: they could pluck ten paragraphs of crisp copy from a 100-page report of yawning verbiage; they could scan a correspondent's copy and unerringly spot the point of it in the last paragraph; on the telephone they could coax quotes from statues; they could survey pillage or massacre and dictate an early story without taking a note.

If speed had been of the essence in King's Lynn and Sheffield then lightning was the rule now. Your story had to be finished by 4 pm because the *Mirror* didn't print in Manchester; copy was transmitted to London where it had to be set in type ready to be transported by rail later that evening. Every day the *Mirror,* unlike the other nationals, failed to carry late-breaking news; but this didn't seem to affect its rising circulation.

But pity the gunman who ran amok in Leeds or Newcastle. Unless he shot at least five people he had no chance of meriting a special edition flown north from London.

The reporting team consisted of Tom Brennan who later graduated to television — *This is Your Life,* in particular — Alan Cooper, a red-haired *Mirror* natural, Stan Vaughan, northern crime reporter who seemed to know every detective north of Watford, Maurice Barsby of the deceptively innocent appearance, and Mickie Clayton a lovely girl with a Family Favourites' voice.

Also around at the time, but poised for Fleet Street, was a flamboyant character named Desmond Wilcox who even then acted like the TV personality he was later to become. (He is now a BBC executive married to Esther Rantzen.)

That left Bernard Shrimsley, tall and elegant and, like Wilcox, clearly cast for his future role. And me. What chance did I stand? Shorthand a subject for jest, social attributes confined to being a good listener, principal excursion into national news coverage a smallpox scare followed next day by a denial. But even during those testing three months a small, ferret part of my brain was scheming to get to Fleet Street.

The first test in that dismal building in Hardman Street, a few doors from the noble *Daily Mail* premises, was the weeklies. Tottering piles of them from all over the North. Every Sunday morning we read them in search of *Mirror* type stories missed by local correspondents. If we missed a story there was always the possibility that a vigilant reporter in another national newspaper office might pick it up.

On that first Sunday I discovered an item about a two-headed calf, snipped it out and showed it to Roly Watkins who was in charge. He was very kind but freaks ... well ... leave them to the fairgrounds. I had only been in the office ten minutes and already I had made an idiot out of myself.

At lunchtime we adjourned to one of the two pubs in Hardman Street where I observed the consumption of booze with awe. As an afterthought, a couple of minutes before closing time, everyone ordered sandwiches. Then back to the weeklies.

Half way through the afternoon I was asked to "get a quote from the Admiralty" on a story from a correspondent about the drunken crew of a destroyer that had wrecked a fishing port on the north-east coast during a courtesy call.

I stared at the copy, my mind paralysed. Getting quotes from Government departments is one of the most tedious of journalistic chores. But I had never been asked to get one before: you didn't phone London from Sheffield without getting written permission.

To actually put in a call to the Admiralty ... Who did I speak to? The Admiral of the Fleet? No one seemed aware of my predicament. Stan Vaughan was on the telephone speaking in code to a detective; Alan Cooper had mounted an attack on a typewriter; the pages of the weeklies rustled around me.

I dialled directory inquiries and in a low voice furtively asked for the number of the Admiralty. Armed with the number I stared at the telephone; then Stan, hat on the back of his head, broke off his abstruse conversation and whispered: "Ask for the duty officer."

The duty officer possessed a refined voice and sounded bored to the point of distraction. *"Daily Mirror?"* God, what was he doing talking to the Mirror. "Just a minute I'll make a note of that."

Then, after a long pause — perhaps he'd knocked back a pink gin to prepare himself for the debasement ahead — he said: "What can I do for you, *Mirror*?"

"I'd like your comment on a story."

A yawn reached me from London. "What story's that, *Mirror*?"

"I'll read it to you."

"Do you really have to?"

Ignoring him I began to read. It took a long time.

When I'd finished he said: "Didn't quite catch the last bit. Could you repeat it."

I repeated it aware that I was by now attracting attention in the newsroom.

"How many members of the crew?"

"About fifteen."

"I don't see how it can be *about* fifteen," the duty officer grumbled. "Anyway, *Mirror*, what do you want to know?"

Ah, there he had me. I wasn't at all sure what I did want to know. "Any disciplinary action?" I asked. Beside me Stan Vaughan nodded approvingly.

"No comment, *Mirror*."

"Can you find out?"

"No comment."

We now seemed to be moving into the realms of Gilbert and Sullivan.

A new voice now entered the ludicrous conversation. It was Stan Vaughan's who had picked up an extension. "I assume you do know about the incident," Stan said.

"Hallo, *Mirror*, your voice has changed."

Stan held up his hand to keep me quiet. "Do you know about the incident?"

"Not until you told me about it."

"That's fine," Stan said. "That's great. It so happens that it's

188

reported in every Sunday newspaper in the land. And," Stan continued, "I'm going to quote you."

"Quote me?" Apprehension denting the boredom. "What can you possibly quote me on?"

"Not quote exactly," Stan said, winking at me. "I shall merely say that the one person in Britain who was unaware of a serious incident involving one of Her Majesty's ships was the duty officer at the Admiralty."

A pause. Then: "What exactly was it you wanted to know, *Mirror?*"

"Disciplinary action," Stan said.

"I'll ring you back," said the duty officer. And ten minutes later he did.

The news desk was satisfied with the quote. It wasn't a shattering contribution to the paper but at least it displayed a degree of professionalism. And they weren't to know that it was Stan Vaughan's professionalism.

At 7 pm I returned to my temporary digs at Chorlton-cum-Hardy. My first day on a national had been anti-climactic. But next morning there was compensation. Details of the disciplinary action against the sailors were spread across four columns.

* * *

The summer days lengthened, then began to shorten, and I hadn't yet made my mark. No catastrophes but no inspired strokes to establish me on the permanent staff.

I found a self-contained flat in a small house in Clarence Road in the suburb of Longsight and Elizabeth and Patrick, a beaming extrovert of a baby, moved in.

Most of my assignments were in the smoky towns clustered around Manchester like spawn. Stockport, Salford, Bolton, Rochdale, Oldham, with occasional excursions to Wigan,

Blackburn, Huddersfield or Accrington. Bleak but vital places, driven by pistons and fuelled by furnaces, greenery as sparse as a fig-leaf on a statue.

The most dramatic story I covered in those first few weeks was a tragedy in a cricket pavilion. Spectators and players were sheltering from the rain during a summer storm when lightning struck. Two of the spectators were killed.

The *Daily Mail* sent a reporter who was to become one of Fleet Street's finest writers. His name was Vincent Mulchrone, a journalist with that rare gift of converting his own humour and compassion into prose. He was a big man, a lovely man, and he died in 1977 far too young.

I met him outside the stricken pavilion; we made our notes and raced for telephones. It was a big story and I dictated about three pages.

In the paper next morning the story made two paragraphs. It was Coronation Day.

* * *

But, irrespective of whether I was making any impression on Jack Clarke, I was certainly learning refinements of my trade. In particular the delicate techniques of interviewing. The public's reaction to a call from the Press is rarely lukewarm: they either usher you to the best armchair or try and disarrange your features with the front door. If the reaction is hostile then there is hope: there's a story there somewhere.

While waiting for assignments I spent much of my time in Hardman Street listening to the experienced reporters conducting interviews by telephone. Mickie Clayton was probably the best exponent. She would hold the receiver away from her ear while a voice rose to splenetic fury at the other end of the line. As the voice faltered into incoherence she would whisper huskily: "I quite agree with you, I would have done exactly the same." A mystified pause; if you throw a bottle of vitriol you don't expect the victim to condone the crime. A few minutes later the voice, if it were male, would be asking for her telephone number.

I also discovered that a terse negative can be used to effect. "Mr. Maltravers, did you in fact know that the girl with whom you eloped to Gretna Green was a ward of court?"

Reply: "No."

Introductory paragraph to the story: Henry Maltravers last night denied etcetera.

And I learned the art of brevity in which the *Mirror* excelled. It is in fact far more difficult to condense a story into eight succinct, well-balanced paragraphs in a tabloid newspaper than it is to let yourself run to a column in the *Daily Telegraph*.

Alan Cooper was a master of this craft. He suggested one day that I adjourn for a beer, but I was immersed in a report on an outbreak of food-poisoning compiled by a master of obscurity.

Journalists are not by nature solitary drinkers and he sat in front of me fidgeting while I tried to digest some of the more disgusting details of the outbreak.

Finally he said: "Have they traced it to one person?"

"A kitchen-maid at a canteen as far as I can make out."

"Her hands?"

I nodded.

"That's your intro then. One pair of guilty hands ... "

I joined him for a beer ten minutes later.

Pubs, in fact, are the second offices of reporters; ideal for conducting interviews, writing stories, phoning copy and recounting the masterly strokes you have just pulled. And Manchester was well served with pubs sympathetic to a journalist's needs. In fact one, kept by an insomniac, stayed open all night, placating patrolling constabulary by leaving a jug of ale on the window-sill.

If you weren't one of this particular pub's furtive patrons there was always the Press Club. But on £15 a week I hadn't yet aspired to a bar where, in the early hours of the morning, editors such as the *Daily Express's* legendary "Strangler" Lewis drank, and large whiskies were the order of the night.

One of the Press Club habituees was a reporter on one of the two evening papers, the *Evening Chronicle,* a tabloid, and the *Evening News,* a text-sized paper, locked in healthy competition. Evening paper journalists are a different breed to morning newspapermen, their attitudes conditioned by having to get out of bed at horrendous hours to fill editions which are on the streets by mid-morning.

After a marathon session this particular reporter arrived home in the cold light of dawn. Cautiously he slid the key in the front-door lock, stealthily he climbed the stairs avoiding steps that creaked. Then he sat on the end of the bed where his wife lay asleep and began to take off his shoes.

At which point his wife awoke, sat up in bed and said: "Hallo, darling, what time is it?"

Her husband replied: "Five-thirty, darling. Just off." Tied up his shoe-lace and left the house.

But my budget rarely allowed me to be home late. And the evenings were spent listening to the radio, practising shorthand and worrying whether I would be given a staff job because by now there were only three weeks of my trial left.

XXII

Two stories strengthened my claims to permanent employment.

The first was a murder. A Pole had been found stabbed to death in the basement of a seedy lodging house in one of the towns camped round Manchester.

The story looked as though it would merit a maximum of two paragraphs. In the first place the murder had all the hallmarks of squalor which neither "dramatic developments" nor police raids could disperse; in the second the dead man was a foreigner which stultified editorial interest unless he was a dope-peddlar, a playboy or Nazi war criminal. One or two races such as French, American or Red Indian were exempt from this generalisation, but Polish wasn't one of them.

It was a dull news day and I was dispatched in the office car, a black Humber Hawk, with driver and photographer. There were three photographers on the *Mirror's* Manchester staff: Ernie Chapman who wore blazer and flannels and always looked as if he were bound for the nineteenth hole; Joe Bottomley, a smallish man whose mild manners deceived many a reluctant subject; and Tom Lyons, a competent rough diamond, who once scooped an unconcerned world with a picture of my son Patrick, and a teddy bear which was published in a couple of northern editions.

None of the other nationals bothered to send a staffman and

it was with a disturbing fusion of pomposity, engendered by the gleaming limousine and driver, and acute anxiety that I arrived at the scene of the murder.

The street was the familiar parade of terrace cottages featured in every movie about the North Country or Welsh mining communities. It was Sunday afternoon and, apart from a dozen or so children playing cricket against a wall with a home-made bat, it languished in post-luncheon torpor. The sun warmed the black walls of the houses and the sky was a blue canal between the rooftops, but sunshine seemed incongruous here: the street would only come alive with rain painting light on grey slates, with a wind bowling men to the furnaces and girls to the mill. And the boys with their knee-length shorts and pudding-basin hair-cuts should have been playing on hard clean sand beside the sea.

All in all the street seemed to have been remarkably phlegmatic about the murder.

One of the boys fielded the hard rubber ball and looked at me suspiciously. "Art thou a copper?"

"Do I look like one?"

"Aye," said the young Len Hutton, "thou does."

This hadn't occurred to me before. It was the height, I supposed, and the feet. Or perhaps any stranger hereabouts was presumed to be a policeman.

"Well, I can assure you I'm not."

"Don't thee talk funny."

"Aye," I said manfully, "I suppose I do." And while he wiped his nose with the back of his hand and considered this I asked: "Do you know where the, ah, incident was?"

"You mean't murder?" as though he was talking about a game of marbles.

"Aye, that would be it."

"Then thou art a copper."

"I'm a reporter," I said.

"Which paper?"

"*Mirror.*"

"Give us thruppence then."

Furtively I handed him a threepenny-bit aware that in our society it wasn't advisable to be seen giving children money.

"Where was murder then?"

"Down there," pointing to the end of the street where the cottages suddenly rose two and three-storey high. "Where policeman's standing outside, dafty."

I walked with dignity to the end of the street and stared at the tenement. There wasn't much background colour here — an area furnished with overflowing dustbins, flaking paintwork, yellowing curtains hung by string, not a drop of blood.

The policeman said: "Good afternoon, sir, can I help you?"

"I'm from the Press."

"Got a pass then, have we?"

I shook my head.

"Best be on your way then, lad."

Would I still have been *sir* with a pass?

I interviewed one or two neighbours who supplied the usual information that he was a man who kept himself to himself. They were also convinced that he had been drunk and had been stabbed by "the old slag" he was living with. Not front page stuff; no international intrigue here; no blondes "known to Royalty" being held for questioning.

A Ford Popular pulled up and a small man with thinning hair and a tooth-brush moustache climbed out. He said to me: "You from *Mirror?*"

I said I was.

"Thought as much. Only bugger which hasn't ordered a story," indicating that he was the local freelance covering for the rest of the nationals.

He walked over to the policeman who greeted him as though they were talking over their garden fence. They glanced at me, nodded knowingly and talked in whispers for five minutes.

Then the freelance sauntered over to me and remarked: "Bloody good story, isn't it?"

No remark can be more calculated to instil despair into the reporter who can see no gleam of a story than this simple observation.

"Not bad," I said.

"Have you got pictures?"

"Oh yes, we've got pictures." Of what? I wondered. My photographer had taken a picture of the house and the street's nameplate and retired to a cafe at the end of the street.

"Smashing," he said. "Best find a telephone and get this lot over." I noticed a thick wad of notes in his hand. "Bloody good story." He climbed into the Popular and was gone.

I gazed up and down the heat-exhausted street while steel bands of hopelessness tightened around my chest. Bloody good story? A drunken Pole who kept himself to himself stabbed by "an old slag." What the hell had the freelance unearthed?

I went to the police-station but the detectives assigned to the murder were out on the case. And, being Sunday afternoon, I wouldn't find them in the pubs — or, if they were in the pubs, no landlord was going to open the doors to me. Morosely I returned to the street where the scene was unchanged.

But no. At the far end of the street two men in grey suits were knocking at doors, working their way methodically in my direction. Detectives making door-to-door inquiries. It didn't inject fire into the story but it helped.

I approached one of the detectives who looked as hot and dispirited as myself. "How's it going?" I asked.

"It isn't." He was sturdy, prematurely bald, as easily identifiable as a policeman as a bobby on traffic duty. "And who might you be?"

I told him but, unlike so many policemen in that era, he didn't go into a recitation about seeking information through the normal channels. "This is a dicey one, squire," he said, lighting a cigarette.

"Is it?" I noticed that his accent wasn't northern and I tried out my limited social graces. "You're not from these parts?"

"Dead right, I'm not. I'm from the Smoke. And you?"

"Muswell Hill. That's north London . . . "

"You don't have to bloody tell me. I was born there."

We surveyed each other in astonishment while cameraderie bloomed. "Well I'll be damned," I said. "What school . . . ?"

"Tollington," he interrupted.

"Me too."

"Well, we must have a pint one day. Meanwhile I've got to get on with this bloody chore."

"Any leads?" I asked.

"Not as far as I know." He tossed his cigarette away. "He was a snout, you know. A police informer."

I didn't know; but I did know a story when I heard one. I wondered if he could see me quivering. Casually I remarked: "Gangland vengeance?"

He looked at me quizzically, then smiled. "Something like that, squire. And there's a couple of funny angles, too. You see he was run over by a car before he was stabbed." He smiled again. "Now work that one out."

We shook hands, vowed to have that pint some day and went our separate ways, two old Tollingtonians who not so many summers ago had played in our green blazers on the lawns of Alexandria Park.

I retired to the cafe where the photographer sat staring at a scummy cup of tea. "Nothing in it?" he asked.

"Oh yes," I said, "there's something in it all right," and told him.

"Christ," he said and set off down the road.

The intro materialised instantly in my brain and flowed into the lead of my pencil. It wasn't brilliant — in fact it was written to formula — but it was crisp and neat:

Police were last night investigating the Mystery of The Man Who Was Murdered Twice.

It was the front page lead and none of the other nationals had a smell of it. I hoped the freelance with the Ford Popular enjoyed reading it.

* * *

By now I had moved into the last week of my trial but nothing was said about my future. Jack Clarke had departed to set up his own freelance agency in the north-east and Roly Watkins had taken over as news editor. I hovered round the news desk like a worried husband in a maternity home. I stared at him in the pub until he buried his head in his pint, but there was no response — although in his charming way he treated me as if I was staff and that was my only foothold of hope.

I wondered if Bernard Shrimsley had heard anything, but Bernard was inscrutable, operating with the same awesome authority that he had displayed since his arrival. I became neurotic, imagining a clandestine meeting between Roly Watkins and Bernard in which Bernard's appointment was confirmed and "poor old Lambert's" failure was gently derided.

At home the tension was having its effect. I shouted at Patrick who chuckled all day and bawled all night; I scowled at my dinner and complained to the tenants above us about their habit of shifting furniture at 1 am. The complaint was a mistake because they were rich enough to own a TV with a screen the size of a postcard and, until then, they had invited us upstairs to watch *Fabian* or *What's My Line?*

I didn't know whether to pay another month's rent in advance or retire gracefully to Devon and take up crime. In the evenings we walked Patrick in a dried-up park nearby and discussed the future with melancholy relish.

Then I had my second break.

Sadly, the story was all too common: an old lady had died unnoticed, unwanted, unmourned. The only evidence of death was the number of unopened milk bottles on the door-step. But journalistically the case was elevated by the remarks of the coroner who said that the old lady might still have been alive if the neighbours had taken the trouble to visit her. The obvious follow-up was to interview the neighbours.

It wasn't a picture story, the office car was in use and I made the lone journey to the suburb on the outskirts of Manchester by bus and train. It was a pleasant enough area, neat houses and trim gardens, not the usual setting for such stories.

A freelance had preceded me and the neighbours didn't appreciate being tackled twice on the same sorrowful subject. Some reacted belligerently, others offered excuses rehearsed since the freelance's visit. One remarked that in the event of my death the milk-bottles would probably reach the pavement before anyone would bother to investigate.

The break was provided by an old man in shirt-sleeves puffing a pipe. He said: "And just who the hell does he think he is?"

"Who?"

"The coroner, of course."

I looked at him blankly.

The old man took his pipe from his mouth, regarded the smoke dribbling from the stem and smiled the complacent smile of those possessing knowledge of inestimable value.

"You mean you didn't know?"

"Know what?" I was seized by an urge to grab his pipe and smash it on to the door-step.

"Come on, you must know."

"Sir, I . . . do . . . not . . . know . . . "

"Well, well, well." He chuckled at the naivety of the Press. "Fancy that," he said, knocking out a wad of wet ash from the bowl of his pipe. "Well I'll be darned," he remarked.

I glanced at my watch. "I haven't much time."

"Deadline to beat, eh, young man?"

The only object worth beating, I thought savagely, was his silly old head. "Five minutes to go," I told him.

"And you really don't know about the coroner?"

"No." Was he perhaps a transvestite?

"Why, he lives just up the road. You could say he's one of the neighbours he criticised."

Retreating down the garden-path at a backward canter, I thanked him and belted down the road to the coroner's house. It wasn't in the same street but it was only round the corner.

No, the coroner told me, he hadn't realised how close he lived when he had reproached the old lady's neighbours. And he weighed in with a lot more superb quotes.

Once more adrenalin raced in my veins. I telephoned the office, gabbled excitedly to someone on the news desk and dictated a story direct from my notes. Something to the effect: *A coroner who rebuked neighbours for allowing an 80-year-old widow to die alone and friendless last night discovered that he lived only 100 yards away.*

The story was exclusive and made a page lead. I was congratulated. But still no one said anything about a permanent job.

Over a lunch-time pie and pint that day Roly Watkins said: "By the way you'll be getting another two quid a week."

"I will?"

200

"Well you are on the staff," he said.

I took a deep swallow of beer, choked and sprayed him with froth.

He looked at me with concern. "I did tell you, didn't I?"

I shook my head distributing the froth around the bar.

"Oh dear. I was supposed to have told you a fortnight ago. Still, not to worry. You haven't been worrying, have you?"

"Worrying? Good God no," I said.

* * *

After a celebration glass of stout with Elizabeth, I immediately began to plan the next phase in my campaign to reach Fleet Street. But now it was even trickier than before. I owed everything to the *Mirror*, and what's more I wanted to stay on a paper whose professionalism earned respect among all journalists. But you can't manoeuvre within an organisation without your immediate superiors knowing. What then was I to do?

For a few months I traversed the North Country. Stood in for Rupert Morters, the *Mirror* man in Newcastle, after he had been in a road accident; spent a few days in Liverpool with its legendary press club where every night was like a docker's wedding reception.

Then Elizabeth's mother who lived in Dartford, Kent, was taken seriously ill. To her Manchester was Siberia: she would have died if she had been transported there. The only solution was to move to London to be near her.

I told Roly Watkins who told Ken Hord, that austere disciplinarian who nosed out lies like a dog trained to find truffles. But not austere when family troubles surfaced, when compassion was needed. One month later I was transferred to Fleet Street, arriving there just over three years since I had faced a bewildered schoolmaster and asked: "Do you consider, Sir, that a diet of fish enhances the capabilities of the brain?"

All Futura Books are available at your bookshop or newsagent, or can be ordered from the following address:
Futura Books, Cash Sales Department,
P.O. Box 11, Falmouth, Cornwall.

Please send cheque or postal order (no currency), and allow 25p for postage and packing for the first book plus 10p per copy for each additional book ordered up to a maximum charge of £1.05 in U.K.

Customers in Eire and B.F.P.O. please allow 25p for postage and packing for the first book plus 10p per copy for the next eight books, thereafter 5p per book.

Overseas customers please allow 40p for postage and packing for the first book and 12p per copy for each additional book.